THUG LOVE

THUG LOVE

Why Women Are Attracted to Bad Boys

Turning Risky Behavior into
Responsible Behavior

Dr. Raymond D. Petty, Ph.D.

Library of Congress Control Number:		2014915648
ISBN:	Hardcover	978-1-4990-6862-7
	Softcover	978-1-4990-6863-4
	eBook	978-1-4990-6864-1

This book was printed in the United States of America.

Rev. date: 10/14/2014

To order additional copies of this book, contact:
Xlibris LLC
1-888-795-4274
www.Xlibris.com
Orders@Xlibris.com
650648

Contents

Dedicated to my loving father, Raymond Petty (Big R);
my forever-humorous brother Ronald Petty;
and my baby-girl daughter Shanee Petty-Jackson,
all of whom went on before me during the seven-year period
this project was being researched.

And last, but surely not least, Malvina Petty, a Mom who is
the most amazing woman I have ever known.

PREFACE

Help Wanted! Help Wanted! Help Wanted! At every stop along this most enlightening journey, I would see this sign over and over again. To be clear, this was not a Help Wanted sign in the conventional sense. It would not be on an oversized billboard, or in the classified ads, or on a neon sign parked in the window of a business or a store. It was in the eyes, in the expressions, and in the body language of the hundreds of women I spoke with on the subject of why so many women are attracted to bad boys. And through these eyes, the expressions, and the body language, the many stories told came alive, and they did so in such a compelling manner that I ended up spending more than seven years researching this phenomenon.

What started out as simple inquiries quickly took hold of my attention and wouldn't let go. After all that I had seen and heard over these years, I would have no inner peace until I did everything I could to shed light on and bring to the forefront what is clearly one of the most, if not *the* most, problematic of interpersonal relationships and lifestyles in our society today. One thing is for sure: there was no shortage of women holding up the Help Wanted signs, looking for a way out of thug love. White women, black women, Hispanic and mixed women, women from Africa, a woman from South America, a Native American woman, a woman with roots in the Middle East, and a woman from the LGBT community would all volunteer to share their stories. They would recount their bad boy experiences in large- and small-group discussions, through surveys, and as case studies. And to the credit of these brave women, not one of them had a problem sharing their stories on the record.

Something very special was unfolding right before my eyes. It was like the final parts of a puzzle coming together to reveal for the first time the complete and whole picture. But this would not be the completed picture of a flower or an animal but rather a picture of life in real time, in the fast lanes of questionable and dangerous relationships. Not only were these real-life personal stories of women in thug love compelling, but the number of volunteers, along with, and perhaps even more importantly, the diversity of those who shared their story, would be a game changer—elevating these simple inquires and observations into extensive research and eventual reporting.

As the initial research began, it soon became evident that women's attraction to bad boys transcended race, culture, ethnicity, and socioeconomic status. There are countless stories in magazines; on the Internet, through social media; and other print outlets of women of all stripes who have had some experience, either directly or indirectly, with bad boys. This includes rich women, middle class women, and women of modest means; professional and executive women; women in sports; and even women celebrities. I often recall having lunch with a well-to-do white executive woman to discuss my book and the research on this topic. It turned out that she was waving a Help Wanted sign herself, but it was for her daughter who was dealing with a bad boy. It was obvious that this bothered her considerably as she was looking for a way out of thug love for her daughter.

These realities played a major role in inspiring me to continue delving deeper into this investigation. In fact, it was the transcending nature of this bad boy phenomenon that would seal the deal for my completion of this research, which I eventually began referring to as a "help has arrived" mission. After all, the prevailing purpose for writing this book—reaching and helping as many women as possible—was now within reach. No matter where they lived, what they did, or who they were, there was a story for every woman, a story that every woman could relate to. And make no mistake about it: when women begin to relate to each other, especially when the topic is relationships, men might want to watch their backs. The bond and connection between women can sometimes be so powerful that one woman's story becomes another's. And within this paradigm, women begin to get it and not just sense a need to change directions but actually begin the process.

There were both good news and bad news as I went forward with my "help has arrived" mission. Most people want the bad news first. So the bad news was that it was impossible for me to listen to hours upon hours of recounts of the "lived experiences" of women in thug love and not see and feel the pain and suffering in their eyes. The numerous stories of the absence or loss of self-worth was deeply embedded in their expressions, and the profound sense of helplessness, disrespect, and of course abuse was in their verbal and nonverbal body language—all at the hands of bad boys. But the good news was the redeeming value of experiencing these recounts because through these experiences, I was rewarded with a deeper insight into the complex emotions women experience with interpersonal relationships in general and with these bad boys specifically. And now, armed with this insight, I was in the position to turn what was rapidly becoming mainly a book of problems into a book of solutions as well.

Self-help strategies work best when presented in easy-to-understand and down-to-earth terms. This would have its challenging moments because a considerable amount of statistical data would be necessary to do justice to this research. And statistical data and down-to-earth terms are not always an easy mix. But being a firm believer that "straight talk walks," finding the correct balance between the two was a must. To meet this challenge, there were three goals I would be every mindful of and always keep before me as I put in writing all that I had learned.

The first goal was to be factual. There is no better way to "keep it real" than to present the facts and nothing but the facts. To remain true to this goal, it was most imperative for me not to present the facts as a research paper but rather as a "lived experience" paper. In other words, be the messenger, just the messenger. Let the voices of the women speak for themselves. This was particularly noteworthy because there is not a lot of extensive research-based information written on this topic—especially comprehensive books containing case studies, surveys, and other factual content. Therefore, the more women's voices are heard, the more facts; the more facts, the more helping strategies; and the more helping strategies, the more rescues from bad boys.

My second goal was to educate. At the end of the day, women's attraction to bad boys is a mindset issue that more often than not is emotionally driven rather than thoughtfully appraised. The resulting behavior usually finds the woman getting involved in relationships that are going nowhere—dead-end relationships. Changing this behavior means changing this mindset, changing this thinking. I often look at it as liberating one's mind, and to educate is to liberate. But while change is a constant, resistance to change is common. So whatever approach I would use to educate, it had to convey a convincing and persuasive message—a message that the liberating power of knowledge can and will free any woman from thug love's tangled web of deception, distrust, and disrespect if they so desire. A basic understanding of the psychology of women's attraction to these bad guys is the educational tool that will bring about this liberation and thus open the mind to change. Let me quickly add: this will not require one to become a psychology major, just psychology minded. And learning to do so on this most basic level will be like having a silent friend in the room when activating some of the self-help tips that are forthcoming. A brief example may be helpful here. Every time a woman allows the bad boy to have his way, she is *reinforcing* his behavior—a term used in psychology to describe one of the many ways behaviors are shaped and eventually acted out. Just understanding this concept from a psychological perspective moves it from an emotional process to a cognitive or thinking process. And it is when we begin to think that we have the best chance to change our behavior. Guess what? You just had a simple lesson in basic psychology. And now you can use this most basic education to liberate and thereby activate your inner self to change.

The third and final goal was to be a vehicle of inspiration. The facts are necessary because they prepare the mind to be open to be educated, and the education is the launching pad which elevates one's thinking to higher levels of action. While these two processes are interacting, the inspiration and motivation to change begin to take flight. There is no doubt that as women's voices are raised through their own lived experiences, the path of many women from all walks of life will be brightened. And this light is the inspirational breakthrough which will encourage and motivate them to discover or rediscover any lost sense of hope, independence, or self-reliance of which they were robbed while dealing with bad boys. And as this becomes more and more of a reality, the Help Wanted signs will become hard to find. What can be more inspirational than having at your disposal the blueprint, the knowledge, and the tools to move from doubt to stability, from abuse to civility, and from chaos to tranquility?

CHAPTER 1

The Phenomenon Observed

There are events or moments in most of our lives that grab our attention in a unique or special kind of way. These moments stand out in such a manner that while they may not elevate to the level of life changing, such events almost surely change the way we look at certain aspects of life. In our constantly growing high-tech society, many of us would be tempted to capture such moments on our cell phones, tablets, or the latest such state-of-the art devices. On another level, however, it has become clear that attention-grabbing moments may very well motivate, inspire, or even encourage us to respond in ways that are as unique or distinctive as the events or moments are themselves.

I experienced one of these attention-grabbing events the first day on campus while entering the building where I was about to teach my opening class in general psychology. It was very noticeable that most of the girls standing outside the building (and there were quite a few) were talking to guys who looked a little rough around the edges. Highly visible were such things as chains around their necks, not the small chains but the oversized nature, many smoked cigarettes, and most flaunted their signature baseball caps, of course, with the front turned to the back. Needless to say, they were heavily tattooed, and you could be sure that a good number of these guys wouldn't be caught dead without their pants pulled halfway down their behinds. Well, let me keep it real and just say what I was really thinking, and that is "Wow! These guys look like thugs or, at the very least, bad boys." The body language alone of these guys as they interacted with the girls looked pimpish. And the behavior of the girls was most revealing as well. If I didn't know any better, the majority of these young ladies almost seemed to be in some type of trance or a hypnotic state as they socialized with these guys. Perhaps another way of describing this would be that the girls treated these guys as though they were some kind of rock stars. Speaking of body language, the young women appeared to be so accommodating and submissive that I thought to myself, *This is dangerous.* Don't they understand that this kind of behavior, especially to this extent, is not only risky but could also easily place them in harm's way? Someone needs to point out to these young ladies that such obliging and vulnerable behavior is most likely responsible for many of the cases around the country, and even the world for that matter, where women have been abused, abducted, raped, and even worse. Men can read and often prey on these weaknesses of women. But while the average bad boy is not likely to go to this extreme, no woman can afford to take a chance to find out.

The scene I just described was not necessarily new to me because I've seen very similar bad boy behavior play out quite frequently at the high school where I also teach. What made this memorable was seeing the same basic scene in an undergraduate college campus as well. And even more intriguing was the fact that not only were the age groups different, nineteen to twenty-one and often higher versus fifteen to eighteen, but also the high school was predominantly black while the college was predominantly white.

Reflecting on all that was observed, there was a growing sense of enthusiasm and excitement that perked me up, causing me to go into research mode. For someone with an investigative mind, this can be a good thing. It's a lot like a reporter who smells a story. Nothing can get a researcher or reporter's adrenaline flowing like sensing there's an important human-interest story or a social question out there that if answered could greatly benefit society. I recall my first graduate-school advisor, teacher and mentor, Dr. Rhonda Jeter, once telling me that studying the behavior of people can become addictive. The truth of this quickly manifested itself in me because investigating thug love soon became a routine part of my life, which continues to this day.

Initially, two questions came to mind: Why are students on a college campus behaving in basically the same manner as the students at a high school? And what is it about this dangerous craze that is so appealing that women are such willing and active participants? I would later find out that the answer to these and many related questions were extremely insightful and would permanently change the way I would view these dicey types of relationships.

The next thing that happened came out of curiosity first and then frustration at what had been observed while entering the building. I walked into my psychology class and after getting the students settled down I couldn't help but to ask, "What is it about these bad guys that are so attractive to you ladies?" I didn't realize at the time that this one question would usher in one of those special moments that would send me on a fact-finding, eye-opening, multiyear research project. The passion and intensity with which this issue was discussed in response to my initial question was most enlightening. The nature and scope of the dialogue revealed that interpersonal relationships were constantly at the forefront of most of my students' minds. It was surprising to see students who, as it turned out, rarely participated in class conversations, discussing this issue with such a high level of input, passion, and enthusiasm. *What an excellent platform to teach psychology* was a prevailing thought in my mind. This would later turn out to be proven correct. By framing and discussing some of the principles of psychology in context of interpersonal relationships, a much higher degree of comprehending this discipline was achieved by many of my students. As the dialogue continued and more views were shared, it became even clearer that I would have to dig deeper and research this phenomenon further to better understand its impact on today's women specifically and dating in general. It also became clear, from the tone and emotions displayed, that many of these young women were actually reaching out for a better understanding of their own behavior as well. From the intensity and body language of the initial thug love participants, one could easily sense their confusion, pain, fear, the results of rejection and no small amount of misguided thinking. Once again, I reflected to myself, *What a unique opportunity.* And as I considered the high level of passion and very strong feelings displayed by so many, it became clear that the attention-grabbing moment that would inspire and propel me into extensive research on this phenomenon was indeed upon me.

Interpersonal relationships on almost any level are often emotionally and psychologically taxing. Few of us will escape the strains and stressors that are so frequently associated with intimate social relationships. This is especially true in today's atmosphere of instant communication and gratification and of course, the growing impact of social media. The fact that the divorce rate in our country is approaching or by some accounts has reached a staggering 60 percent or more confirms how far-reaching the emotional and psychological impact of relationships can be. Further evidence can be found in countless self-help books, endless magazine articles, and the growing number of television and radio shows devoted to this very sensitive subject. Trying to keep relationships afloat, or attempts to mend those that are falling or have fallen apart, almost seems like a full-time job in our culture, and this is just for the more conventional type of relationships—if there were such a thing as a conventional relationship these days. When you factor in the high-stake, ever-present dangers of thug love, the psychological and emotional damage is easily double that of the so-called traditional relationship. Thus, the feelings of helplessness, hopelessness, vulnerability, and even shame, which are commonly associated with the typical union, are often augmented to a traumatic level in thug love. Since the fallout of thug love is bound to produce psychological and emotional damage, it is most beneficial to examine it from the psychological perspective. This serves as a constant reminder that changing the risky behavior of thug love will be a formidable challenge. However, challenges simply present opportunities. And we will use these opportunities to overcome the dangers and obstacles associated with undependable and unreliable relationships

While listening and learning some of the initial dynamics associated with dealing with bad boys, I came to view it as much more than a phenomenon. Whether it was a classroom discussion, a voluntary small-group discussion, or a one-on-one interview, it became apparent that life with bad boys was and remains a reality that is lived out every day in many women's lives. The fear, doubt, and misguided thinking which consistently resurfaced through the expressed experiences of women clearly crystallizes this point. Let there be no doubt: a lot of women have paid and will continue to pay a heavy emotional and social price as a result of dealing with these guys. The picture that has been painted with the words of so many women was not only informative but instructive as well. This representation of life in the thug love lane became the blueprint for the direction I would take in trying to help women discard their Help Wanted signs. And this blueprint initially called for a profile or description of the bad boy.

Imagery can be a powerful way of disclosing or unveiling the "real deal." The physical and behavioral characteristics of people, especially those that present a potential danger to the lives of those involved, can be like a lifeline thrown out to pull someone to safety. Thus, breaking down this phenomenon by first profiling the bad boy was a prudent starting point in developing strategies and interventions to transform this risky behavior into responsible behavior.

CHAPTER 2

The Profile Of The Bad Boy

A combination of emotions triggered the development of the profile of the bad boy. Perhaps it was simply curiosity, the desire to help, intrinsic motivation and determination, or a combination of all of these, but from the initial discussions on the subject of thug love, it would be difficult to move forward without knowing specifically what we were dealing with—what the bad boy really looks like. After all, we are talking about a real person, someone who lives, communicates, and interacts in our communities every day. They may be bad boys, they may not do right by women, but they are not invisible. We cannot afford to act like they exist only in the abstract because in the real world they do. And the fact that interpersonal relationships and dating are so dramatically impacted by these guys only further necessitates putting a face on these individuals. For the many women who are in relationships with bad boys and want out, as well as the many women who want to avoid these unions altogether, developing a real-life description of these guys (attitude, mannerism, patterns, etc.) will be most beneficial. How beneficial, you ask? Just think about it in these terms: with a profile of the bad boy, those who want to avoid having such an encounter will now have a picture they can put on their bedroom wall and mark a great big X across it. On the other hand, women who are currently involved with these deceitful and often conniving males can use their profile as an incentive to develop and activate their strategy to cut their losses.

So what are some of the characteristics of a bad boy? How is he described by women? How does he describe himself? How does he view and treat women? Is he dependable? Does he have a respectable job? Is he trying to better himself? After pondering these questions, it was time to determine the best ways to obtain information in a credible and reliable manner. I recall my mother once telling me that when you want to know something, just ask, but in doing so, make sure you go straight to the source—the people who can provide the truth and the facts. As usual, Mom's advice was the best because I did just what she said and as a result acquired what we in the field of psychology or the behavioral sciences sometimes refer to as "rich information."

To begin with, the research included both women and men, but mostly women. The gender breakdown was approximately 85 percent women and 15 percent men. Nearly 750 surveys were acquired over the period the research was conducted. About 80 percent of these were written surveys, with the remainder being taken by show-of-hands surveys in group sessions, and documented. The participant breakdown for the surveys is as follows: approximately 250 undergraduate students, 150 graduate students, 100 high school students, and approximately 100 nonstudent participants. Throughout the data-gathering process, additional information was obtained from one-on-one interviews, in-depth group-style discussions, and literature reviews on the subject. Summaries of over 150 group discussions were kept in a journal and then transferred into this book. The one-on-one interviews (case studies) were recorded and transcribed. On average, case study interviews lasted between sixty and ninety minutes, and most group discussions would last for at least two hours, sometimes more. Group discussions continue to this day. It is important to remember that most of the data-gathering information in this research contain the "lived experiences" of women who actually dealt with bad boys.

There were ten questions on the survey that provided a well-rounded and serviceable profile of the bad boy. Three of the ten questions received the highest percentages of agreement. From this, it became evident that (1) the bad boy is most likely to disrespect women, (2) he will most likely have had some dealings with the law, and (3) he will most likely have a tattoo. All percentage breakdowns pertaining to the survey data will reflect high school–age students first, followed by undergraduate, graduate, and finally, nonstudent participants. Therefore, the percentages for the first group of questions above are 87 percent, 88 percent, 90 percent, and 91percent, respectively.

There were three profile questions that received moderately high percentages. These responses indicated that the bad boy will (1) most likely not have a college degree, (2) use street language better than the English language, and (3) be heavily into drugs and alcohol. This works out to 72 percent, 76 percent, 78 percent, and 80 percent, respectively.

Finally, the remaining four questions that received relatively low agreement percentages basically meant that the participants disagreed with the question. This proved to be equally informative because it provided excellent data in a converse-type manner. In this regard, participants disagreed with the notion that (1) the bad boy will not likely have a job, (2) he will have low self-esteem, (3) he will most likely wear a suit and tie, and (4) he will most likely want to get married. The breakdown of percentages of low agreement on this group of questions was 33 percent, 39 percent, 50 percent, and 53 percent, respectively.

In light of the low percentage of agreement on these four questions, it was concluded that bad boys will have some type of job. The discussion on this point became most interesting when on quite a few occasions women asked, "Did the question mean legitimate employment?" Most of the time there would be a little laughter after this statement, but it became clear that almost half of the women actually viewed the bad boy as not being employed in the traditional sense. The low self-esteem question was even more revealing. The high percentage of disagreement on this question translates to the bad boy viewing himself in a very positive manner. According to the majority of women, self-esteem for the bad boy was not an issue. I almost wondered out loud: *What could account for these guys feeling so good about themselves?* It just didn't register with me at that time how a guy could feel good about himself while at the same time having run-ins with the law, disrespecting women, doing drugs regularly, most likely working for low-paying dead-end jobs or worse, and basically hustling for a living or, at the least, hustling on the side. What in the world was I missing here? In trying to find some logic in all this, I relied on my training and began to recognize this as a matter of reinforcement.

Before we go any further, let me say up front that "one size does not fit all" when dealing with the profile of the bad boy. Actually, this would be true when dealing with any type of profiling for that matter. The reason this is important to note at this point is that it would be shortsighted and basically dangerous to dismiss a guy as not being a bad boy because he didn't meet *all* of the profile characteristics. This is not how it works. In most cases, all it takes is for a guy to possess just one of the profile characteristics to put him on the bad boy list. One engaging student pointed out in a discussion that she had a relationship with a guy who had a very good job, an executive job, as a matter of fact. Her point was that this was a case where the person didn't fit the profile. She went further to try to make her case by saying he was also well dressed and well spoken. Again, she was making the argument that this particular individual did not line up with the profile. She seemed to have this "I got you" look on her face. At the same time, her body language seemed to be saying, *Now, how do you rectify this?* I said to the student, "I don't think you realize it, but you are actually helping to make my point." She seemed a little puzzled until I asked a couple of questions. The first question was "Did your well-dressed friend with the executive job have any tattoos?" to which she responded, "I don't think so." I then asked, "Has he ever disrespected women?" And she went silent on me. After a little more silence, she admitted that disrespecting women was an area where he did have a problem. I was curious as to whether she felt that a man who disrespects women qualifies him to be considered a bad boy. She seemed hesitant, perhaps even a little protective, but eventually agreed. I reiterated the fact that she was helping me make my point—that all aspects of the profile of the bad boy will not and does not have to be present to make it relevant. As I said before, one size does not fit all. The profile is to be used as a guide, to be informative, but most importantly, not to be used in an "all or nothing" framework when trying to discern the characteristics of these bad guys.

One last thing should be mentioned about the profile of the bad boy, and that is beware of impostors—"the good guys." Believe it or not, there are men who clearly don't fit the profile but actually try to take on the characteristics normally associated with bad boys. This was a frequent occurrence, especially in the classroom. These guys, the impostors, are so awkward in their clothes and mannerisms that they sometimes trigger inward laughter. From my experience as an instructor, the real bad boys are only casually concerned about their grades while the impostors are more often A and B students. The real bad boys are usually very brief and shallow when they do talk in class while the impostors tend to use good language and display critical thinking skills even when they don't want to. The real bad boys seem very comfortable when wearing sunglasses and turned-around baseball caps even in the classroom while the impostors are almost always uneasy with this behavior. So what's behind this? Why would a decent young man want to be seen as a bad boy? It appears this most likely stems from the fact that the bad boy is so heavily glorified in our society that men will try to transform their good guy characteristics to appeal to and gain the attention of the opposite sex. This is probably due to the news on the street that women gravitate to bad boys, and therefore, good guys will be hard-pressed to get attention from women, especially in public. Just think: thug love is so potent and compelling that it even dictates the behavior of men and perhaps even women who are not naturally inclined to engage in any aspect of this phenomenon. By the way, there are even articles on the Internet on how to be a bad boy.

As the profile data was being collected, three significant factors emerged that provided some additional profile information of the women in thug love. First, approximately 80 percent of all the women surveyed indicated that they were either presently in a relationship with a bad boy or previously had such a relationship. This most certainly confirms how widespread this risky behavior is among women. It was tempting to just stop at this point and ask, "Why do so many females engage in relationships that they know are going nowhere?" I can't recall anything being more puzzling over the years. Unfortunately, belaboring this point was not an option at this time. I had to temper and pace myself to accomplish the greater goal of helping to provide alternatives to this unsafe behavior. With 80 percent of all the women surveyed having had at least one personal experience with a bad boy, it was apparent that collecting reliable information would not be a problem. In fact, since most of the data were based on the lived experiences of these young ladies, securing credible information for this research was not an issue as well. *How fortunate it is to get firsthand reliable information like this* was a recurring thought. From a researcher's perspective, it just doesn't get much better than this.

The second significant factor that was confirmed from this investigation is that thug love is not race- or culture sensitive. This point was made earlier, but confirmation is golden. Actually, the many group discussions and personal interviews revealed that regardless of race, most women tend to think on the same level when the subject is bad boy relationships. For instance, the idea that protection was one of the reasons why women desire relationships with these guys was first presented by white women. In nearly every account, black women either dittoed their white sisters or shared very similar views. The bigger picture here is that thug love clearly seems to transcend race or culture. In a way, I was hoping and looking for some differences with respect to race or culture. Even a slight race or cultural difference would at least necessitate some level of comparative or contrasting analysis and assessment on this subject. Oftentimes some differences can help explain phenomenon. This would not be the case with the data collected. In effect, it became apparent that whites, blacks, Hispanics, and other races were open to or had already experienced thug love. And of equal significance, quite a few of these were interracial relationships.

Finally, the data is even more illuminating when looking at this phenomenon from the perspective of age. When a seventeen-year-old girl and a forty-one-year-old woman present similar experiences from what basically amounts to similar mindsets, the eyebrows of almost any researcher would be raised. For instance, a seventeen-year-old girl in a high school classroom commented, "I think girls probably like bad boys because they are not boring." In a graduate school classroom later on that week, a woman in her early forties said, "I really believe that most women are looking for something exciting and challenging and different." If I had not actually witnessed this, I might have said that the odds of mindsets being this similar between a seventeen-year-old high school student and a graduate school student in her early forties were slim to none. Yet, thanks to the lived experiences of women who openly shared, it was obvious that this style of relationship, and all the uncertainty that comes with it, seems to include a very wide range of ages.

Looking back on the three significant research factors that stood out, it became clear that thug love wielded power, widespread influence, and dominance over the lives of the women who chose this lifestyle. The power is evident in the fact that a significant majority of the women, whether surveyed or not, acknowledged being involved with bad boys. The widespread influence is manifested in the reality of the phenomenon being multicultural and practically ageless. And the dominance is confirmed in how much mistreatment women were subjected to in order to be in a relationship with these alpha males.

CHAPTER 3

The Reasons

Observe these three expressions and store them in your mind: "protection," "a challenge," and "I can fix him." In all of the initial group discussions that took place, these three expressions amounted to the main reasons women said they were attracted to bad boys. And these same three reasons were continually confirmed throughout the years the research was conducted. I distinctly recall the first student who seemed anxious to comment actually say that she was indeed attracted to her bad boy for protection. Not long after that, another student, a slightly older–looking woman, said, "I think women are attracted to the bad boys because they want 'a challenge.'" A little later in the discussion, I asked if there was another reason, and a third student remarked, "I think another reason is because a lot of times women feel 'I can fix him.'" *Fascinating* was the only word that could adequately describe my inner thoughts at that point. These three reasons captured my attention and imagination to the point where they would be the triangular focus of the entire research. This further strengthened my resolve to see where this ultimately leads and to do so no matter how long it takes. I thought to myself: *nobody is going to believe this.* Over the next several years, I tested the accuracy of these three reasons using all the research at my disposal. From a data perspective, 64 percent of the woman agree with a sense of "protection," a very impressive 82 percent agreed that "a challenge" was indeed an attraction, while a whopping 85 percent agreed with the notion that women are attracted to bad boys because they feel "I can fix him." It was somewhat surprising to learn that most of the available literature on this subject also consistently support these three reasons as well.

Follow the reasons! After hearing "protection," "a challenge," and "I can fix him" in nearly every discussion, it became clear that this would be the key—that if I followed and examined these three main reasons, it would lead me closer to unlocking the mysteries that seemed to control such problematic behavior. And breaking down the thinking and the mindset behind these reasons would take me to the promised land of research in unraveling these behavioral mysteries. I dealt with each reason individually and found the need to raise questions, challenge unrealistic thinking, and even invoke judicious and practical assumptions. Due to the complexity of these reasons, I found it prudent to address each of them in separate chapters. There was a certain delight in focusing on the causes in this manner because I was ultimately able to expose the risky behavior in ways that women could see the light at the end of the tunnel and therefore perfect the fight to dispose of the Help Wanted signs.

Initially, the approach used in exploring the thinking was basically an outside-looking-in approach. It was largely based on small- and large-group discussions which provided very important and helpful information but at times was somewhat limited with respect to an inside perspective because you can only get but so much information in a public forum. And with what I had learned thus far, it became clear that I would need an inside perspective as well. This led to taking the research to the next level—case studies. I was somewhat hesitant to go there at first because I knew that this would add a considerable amount of time completing this research. From previous experiences, I knew the level of tedious work that goes into conducting personal interviews. Nonetheless, I weighed time against accuracy, and of course, accuracy won. And even though it did add over two more years to the research, it was well worth it.

Things went viral when I did include case studies into the research mix. Not viral in the Internet sense but rather "research viral." The stories that were told were powerful and commanding. They verified and confirmed. They brought to light how life with bad boys in the real world plays out in an up-front, close, and personal manner. In some instances, they opened up new ways of thinking about this phenomenon. As such, the outside-looking-in view provides direction while the inside view provides details. And as we see how they unfold in the lived experiences of women, the wisdom in following these three main reasons—"protection," "a challenge," and "I can fix him"—becomes very apparent. I like to look at it as the outside-looking-in view is the first encounters of the phenomenon while the inside view, which provides a high-definition picture, is the case studies of the phenomenon.

CHAPTER 4

"Protection"

First Encounters

Protection! You've got to be kidding! After hearing this in the first group discussion about bad boys, I felt like offering my own version of that infamous line by Jack Nicholson when he said to Tom Cruise, "You can't handle the truth," in the movie *A Few Good Men*. In the case of thug love, my comment would have been "You can't handle protection!" or better still, "You don't want to handle protection!" Unfortunately, I didn't say what I was thinking because now in hindsight it would have been most appropriate. As the discussions increased over time, there would be even more reactions and more reflections of what I heard and learned about this phenomenon.

The many responses to the question of why women are attracted to bad boys seemed to always ignite healthy discussions year after year. The nonapologetic declarations of "protection" were most intriguing, but the real surprise was seeing so many women, whether in small or large groups, raise their hands in agreement. To openly admit in a public forum that they were attracted to bad boys for protection just didn't seem like the type of information that would be divulged in any type of group discussion, or classroom setting, especially in light of today's cultural impetus by women to be independent. No matter how many times it was articulated, however, it always seemed a little embarrassing. *Protection* sounds so dependent, so subservient.

Nearly certain it was my male psyche that caused my silently shocked reaction to this unexpected revelation, I immediately fired back, as though I was a boxer throwing a counterpunch, "Protection from what?" But what I thought to be a rather straightforward question brought forth nothing but silence. That's correct: silence! In fact it was very noticeable silence. The kind of silence where you just know something profound is about to unfold—the kind of silence that speaks volumes. And it was this very silence that made it clear that most of the young ladies in these group discussions had not thought through this whole notion of protection. Nonetheless, persistent in my pursuit to clearly grasp what was meant by protection, I pressed for an explanation and repeated, "Protection from what?" Fortunately this time, there was a response to my inquiry. With a mood of apprehension in the air, a brave young lady presented a scenario to answer my question and, in doing so, enlightened me at the same time about this protection attraction. She said that when she goes out to a club or party, she wants her man to be able to protect her in case someone wants to start some trouble. No way did I expect anything close to this as an answer. *Remarkable* would be putting it mildly in describing my thoughts. Cognitively, I wasn't even in the same building as this young lady and probably most of the group. I only hoped that my facial expressions didn't reflect my amazement.

Apparently, it was the perception of the rough-and-tough persona of the bad boy that convinced this young lady that he could provide the type of protection she felt she needed. I quickly canvassed how many people agreed with that statement, and again to my surprise, a sizable majority of the women concurred. After that, a different but confident looking young lady added that bad boys just know how to handle themselves when situations get out of hand. Another great opportunity to teach was written all over this discussion because it provided an occasion to present a different viewpoint—one in which I would strive to encourage more open and diverse ways of thinking on the concept of protection.

When I think of protection, I think of a roof over my head, somewhere or someplace where one feels safe and secure. This was my initial response to all that the group had discussed to that point on this topic. As the dialogue progressed, I made the case that protection should not only be associated with something that may or may not occur, a sort of intangible or abstract idea, if you will, but rather on something concrete, physical, something that one can feel and touch as well. At first, many in the group looked a little puzzled, and then they appeared disarmed—as if someone had just confiscated their cell phones. Others began looking as though they were internalizing or scrutinizing what they had just heard. The group was then directed to Maslow's hierarchy of needs to further clarify my point. It was brought to the attention of all that according to Maslow, our first level of needs is physiological—food, clothing, and shelter. "Sounds like protection to me," I remarked. Accordingly, the second level of needs is referred to as security needs—social security and security against hunger and violence, etc. At this point in the discussion, I admonished the group to notice that the physical needs, the needs that provide concrete, tangible protection, come first in Maslow's widely accepted theory.

Thanks to a considerable amount of participation, the dialogue was truly helping most, if not all, gain a more well-informed perspective of protection. This was evident in the fact that the flow of the group's interaction intensified dramatically. It was apparent that some level of learning was taking place. With the interest and awareness of the group heightened, the goal now was to demonstrate that their version of protection was misguided thinking and that it is this type of thinking that contributes to the risky behavior of thug love.

"How often do you think you would need protection from your bad boy at a club or a party?" "How many of you have actually had such an experience?" In nearly every group discussion on protection I would ask these and similar questions, and almost always there were no responses. There were no takers on such questions because the obvious answer would reveal the level of unrealistic thinking of the part of the responder. Moving forward, I would then usually ask, "How often do you think you will need the Maslow hierarchy type of protection?" Once more, there would be no responses because, again, the obvious answer would expose their previous imprudent thinking. However, at this point, since the answer was obvious and could be used comparatively to modify their mindset, I would quickly interject: "every day and every night, 24/7." The likelihood that you will need protection when going to a club or party every day and every night is simply nonexistent. So based on this most straightforward analysis, what kind of protection do you really need? Do you think the bad boy can provide that most basic level of protection for you? We only need to revisit the profile of the bad boy, and it's as visible as their tattoos that it is most likely these highly pursued males are not in a position to provide adequate protection to anyone, especially well-rounded, twenty-four-hour—food, clothing, and shelter— protection. The main reason for this is that real protection requires revenue—money—and in far too many cases, the bad boy's sources of adequate, appreciable, and—might I add—legitimate income are questionable at best. Furthermore, even if he did have the income to put a roof over a woman's head, the bad boy brand clearly suggests this is mostly out of the question. The best a woman is likely to get is an overnight stay or two. Anything longer than this will seriously cramp the bad boy's style.

First of all, if the bad boy gives even the slightest hint that he is remotely open to a long-term commitment, he knows he is done like a well-cooked Thanksgiving turkey. Not only will this damage his image, but having a woman live with him will prevent him from exploring other options, which is at the top of the bad boy playlist.

And frankly, the bad boy brand is not going for that. On one occasion in a group discussion, a female student blurted out in a very defensive manner, "How can you make that judgment?" She really seemed to be upset with me by coming down so hard on the bad boy. I thought to myself, *Great! If I got to get women a little upset to see the light, then so be it.* This is why the psychological behavioral perspective is so important, I explained to her. In psychology we use research data (in this case the profile, the interviews, the discussions, etc.) to describe, predict, explain, control, and change the thinking behind the behavior. Imagine what and how much can be accomplished using this approach in developing strategies to turn the risky behavior of thug love into responsible behavior—the benefits are practically endless. This is what we do in the field of psychology, and in doing so, we ultimately equip those who desire a behavioral makeover with the skills to help them bring this to fruition. For instance, with the type of data and information we now have before us, we can reasonably predict that the bad boy is too self-absorbed, too egotistical, has too much control, and is having too much fun to make the long-term commitment necessary to provide "real" protection. The bad boy has no interest in providing long-term protection. What is the incentive when he is already getting everything he wants? Although many of the participants in these discussions always seemed to be searching for a comeback response, it would not occur. No one had anything to say. I would even allow more time for them to ponder and think through all that had been discussed, and I would ask several more times to make certain, "Did anyone have any further comments?" Still there was no response. The truth always stands alone.

While the dialogue on protection would usually end at this point, the thinking and introspection would begin because after many of these discussions, there were always students who would approach me and want to have one of those after-the-meeting talks. During many of these conversations, the students would typically say they were glad that we had the discussion about protection because they really didn't think about it in those terms. The general consensus was that such a dialogue will really help them think about this in a different way. I told the young ladies that I appreciated the fact that they stepped up to the plate and that the operative word in their comments was *think*. Thinking is the key to extinguishing or avoiding thug love experiences in their lives. And it's not just any type of thinking but rather discerning on an analytical and critical-thinking level.

I gave them an example. A woman who is trying to get out of a protection relationship might want to rethink and use critical-thinking skills to appraise the obvious connection between protection and control. Any serious attempt to evaluate their behavior on this level will certainly begin with introspection—looking inside oneself. When an honest self-inspection is conducted, the bad choices made will be revealed—they will pop up like toast in a toaster. The good thing about bad choices is that they have markers. It's somewhat amazing, but these markers are the hows, whys, and whens of the bad choices. Is this a healthy type of relationship? Is being controlled by someone on any level healthy? What are the long-term psychological effects of being blindly submissive? Thinking on this level, one must be objective and willing to acknowledge their own bad choices as they will certainly surface when the introspection begins. Nonetheless, by doing so, by thinking on this level, by being open and honest with oneself, a woman will experience a certain degree of liberation from making a lot of unsafe and bad decisions when it comes to bad boys. Of course, this will not eliminate making all bad choices, but it most certainly will minimize the choices that frequently contribute to hazardous behavior.

Another interesting aspect of the protection attraction that emerged from various discussions was two frequently used telltale descriptors: "dominant" and "swagger." "dominant" was used to describe the nature of the protection while "swagger" was used to describe the manner in which the man produces the desired dominance. Taking a closer look at these two descriptors will prove to be very insightful to our mission.

"I want my man to be dominant in my relationship. I want him to take charge, to be the man." Dominance seems to be one of the ways protection is actualized in a lot of women's mindsets. There appears to be a connection between being protected and being dominated. However, this correlation is problematic because it can and usually is interpreted differently between the man and the woman. Far too many men don't see it as being dominant over a situation, like the example of being out at a club or party, but as being dominant over the woman herself. This is right down thug love's alley. Being dominant is being in control, and nothing is more important to the bad boy than being in control. He gets to make all the important decisions in the relationship, which means he has his way. How and why this is viewed as dominant, and subsequently protection by the woman, is clearly irresponsible. There is a school of thought which says a woman who wants to be dominated by a man feels this way because she lacks a firm sense of direction for her own life. The submissiveness and learned helplessness that is surely attached to wanting the man to be dominant almost certainly confirms a link to the woman not having a sense of direction in her life. Sadly, too many women feel more comfortable being a follower, being submissive.

Swagger, or swag, is a physical description of the bad boy. It is often deemed a necessary component of protection. Without swag, most women believe it is not possible for the man to protect them. In search of an even more in-depth description of exactly what swag looked like, responses such as "smooth," "cool," and "a kind of confident walk" were consistently voiced. Taking it a step further, I decided to use myself as an example and have asked in many group discussions over the years, "In your view, do I have what you ladies refer to as 'swag'?" If I knew then what I was getting myself into, I probably would have taken a different approach. Nonetheless, I don't know if I should have been surprised or embarrassed, but the response was usually around 55–45, 60–40, or the highest of 70–30 that I did have swag. I found this most interesting in that this swag survey included both the men and women. A little sidebar investigation on the 30 percent to 40 percent who thought I didn't have swag revealed that it was largely based on the fact I was a college professor. It seemed that education was a major factor in their analysis. The 60 percent to 70 percent of students who thought I did have swag based their view mainly on my outward appearance. They cited mannerisms: the way I walked around the classroom, the way I interacted with the students during discussions, and the fact that I would occasionally dress casually. I should have seen this coming, but this would often be followed by students pointing out to me that in light of the results of the classroom swag survey, it seemed to suggest that I may very well fit at least one of the profile descriptors of a bad boy. This would almost always be followed by boisterous laughter by the students or group participants. Needless to say I was embarrassed, but I kept a straight face as best I could. After collecting my thoughts, I decided to give them the scientific response—I guess I should say *my* scientific response—that in light of several different percentages over time, as well as the fact that many of my students were mostly likely biased because of the student-teacher relationship developed over time, the evidence is not conclusive. While most of the students would give me that "yeah okay" look, I was saying to myself, smiling privately, "I got out of that one." But over time, I would not get off that easy. The queries as to whether I have ever had any personal experience being a bad boy myself would be revisited time and time again during my research, and especially by the ladies. Since so many of those who participated in thug love discussions and interviews were open and transparent, and shared their experiences so freely with me, I felt it was only fair that I provide some level of openness in return. Therefore, in the interest of transparency, I would share this: "In many cases with researchers, they will often research those things in which they have a personal interest directly or indirectly. And that's all you're gonna get out of me on that subject."

Finally, I would be remiss if I didn't point out that a woman's gravitation to the protection of a bad boy is not just psychological. Several researchers in the field of evolutionary psychology and in the area of sex, gender, and reproduction have found that the hormone testosterone in men is linked to more dominant personality traits. This includes such things as outgoing personalities, charm, and similar characteristics. Perhaps this is what women really mean when they speak of swagger. Men who possess these qualities are outwardly confident and dominant and thus attractive to a lot of women. In addition, the evidence shows that there can be a variation of levels of this hormone among men. In other words, there are men with high levels of testosterone as well as men with low levels of testosterone. This could account for why some men are more physically attractive to women than others.

Nonetheless, even if the initial attraction to gain the protection of the bad boy is based on physiology more than psychology, it is the latter where the ultimate or latent damage occurs. Seeking protection from a bad boy is still risky behavior in any way it's appraised because control and dominance leads to learned helplessness, and learned helplessness, especially over long periods of time, ultimately leads to depression. One last thing: whether it's swagger, confidence, or coolness, none of these characteristics can be cashed in at the bank. And the last time I looked, it took more than just these personality traits or characteristics to provide real and lasting protection—the Maslow hierarchy type of protection. Since it is most likely that all the bad boy has to offer, all he has to bring to the table, are these peripheral nonrefundable characteristics—brawn and muscles, swag, and of course, a healthy dose of arrogance—"You don't want to handle protection."

CHAPTER 5

"A Challenge"

First Encounters

You won't get a big argument from me about women wanting "a challenge" in their relationships. What possible harm could come from a woman trying to put a little excitement in the relationship? Even in the hands of the most cynical, challenges present new horizons and often promote new and positive outlooks on life. They almost certainly test the will of individuals and in doing so, challenges help build character. Well, that was my point of view until I came face to face with the first encounters of this phenomenon, and the research began revealing exactly what women genuinely meant by "a challenge." After that, all bets were off. Once again, I was about to have some of the things I had learned about women over time totally destroyed. All of this came about as the descriptors used in the discussions on "a challenge" surfaced. In a world in which I was led to believe that women first and foremost coveted stability and security in their relationships, I soon discovered that such a world had drastically changed or perhaps never existed for many women. For the opportunity to engage with a bad boy, many women have turned in their quest for stability and replaced it with words like *adventure, excitement, unpredictable,* and *danger.* These were the words that were used on all levels of the research to convey what women really meant by "a challenge."

The desire to experience something a little different in a relationships is one thing, but descriptors such as these are another story altogether. While these things may, and I emphasize *may,* provide variety and spice in a non–bad boy relationship, this is not the case with thug love. Just a cursory look at these terms revealed that the women's version of a challenge in thug love had little chance to impact the relationship in a positive manner. Painting a complete and holistic picture from each of these descriptors became necessary to enlighten these ladies on the hazards of this type of thinking and behavior. Defining these terms was the first step. *Adventure* is defined as "a hazardous undertaking." Unusual or suspenseful experiences are yet another way adventure is described. *Excitement* basically means "to elicit a reaction or emotion." *Danger* is defined as "exposure to possible evil, injury, or harm," and *unpredictable* implies the inability to be able to have some idea of what lies ahead. Looking at these definitions individually or collectively is alarming because there is nothing good or positive that can come out of this type of challenge. With definitions like "hazardous," "suspenseful," or "exposure to evil, injury, or harm," there is no plausible reason for anyone to engage in relationships that produce these levels of experiences.

On several speaking occasions, mainly in seminars and group sessions, I would present various published articles in PowerPoint presentations that reflected the personal accounts of individuals who had real-life experiences of "a challenge." Some of these individuals were the authors of the articles themselves. The goal was to get the reaction and response of these women to ascertain to what degree, if any, they could relate to these experiences. In an Internet article by Zondra Hughes entitled "Why Some Girls Prefer Bad Guys," she states, in part, that if you ask most females why they like bad boys they'll say the challenge, the excitement or the thrill of living vicariously.

A little less than half of the women took a mild exception with the "living vicariously" expression, but otherwise they agreed and could relate to the basic intent of the comment. When asked exactly what is meant by *excitement*, the conversation went in several directions. One young lady said it was something that was out of the ordinary while another woman described it as simply being something different. To further get a grasp of this concept, the group was asked whether excitement could mean going to an amusement park or something of that nature. This example drew a rather noncommittal and weak response, but quickly after that question, a different and seemingly frustrated woman suggested that "excitement is something more physical." Asked to further explain, the young lady directly and frankly said that "excitement is having wild sex, and I don't know why everybody is trying to put on a front." Needless to say, expressions of laughter and smiles followed this comment, but the majority seemed to quietly agree with this interpretation although at first they seemed rather reluctant to do so, especially publicly. As the discussion continued, the point was made that bad boys are particularly exciting when they are having sex. "They really know how to turn a woman on," commented one young lady. Another attention-grabbing revelation that surfaced was that a lot of women felt that the excitement of sex was one of the factors that caused them to stay in their relationship with their bad boy. The woman who warned the group about putting up a front obviously couldn't take it anymore and practically jumped out of her seat and said, "Everybody in here knows that sex with a bad boy is the main reason that they stay in these relationships." Although most of the women seemed a little surprised at how continuously candid this lady was, no one would take her on. I wanted to know all about "a challenge," and I was surely getting a full dose. Continuing on, the group was asked to put the author's word *thrill* into some type of context within thug love. There were several variations of what that meant to the women: "bad boys are not boring is what's so thrilling" and "just knowing that he is unpredictable thrills me to death" are two examples. But the one that stuck out the most was "I get a thrill in the fact that I'm happy that he chose me." This was most edifying. Uncovering such valuable insight is always encouraging. This last statement is a testament to thug love's extreme allure, at least when it comes around to a "thrill." Eager to see what additional revelations were on the horizon with respect to the "a challenge" attraction, another comment from the Zondra Hughes article was presented on the screen:

> In many cases, the law of opposites attract applies for the "good girls" who crave a little excitement in their lives and who feel that the bad guys are the only ones who can satisfy them.

One of the first obvious questions from a statement such as this is "Why do so many women believe that only bad boys can satisfy them?" Much to my surprise, a man responded to this inquiry, saying that the man can give the woman "a lifestyle." To illustrate his point, he continued by saying that the "good girl" already has a pretty good life, she has everything, and therefore, she is looking for something different. "If that's true, why would a woman who has such an upside to her life, and obviously has a bright future, want to go on the 'dark side'?" was my comeback response. One of the older women in the group responded before I could even finish asking the question: "Because they know it's wrong. It's like human nature." "But it's so dangerous" was my response. Why would a woman who "has it going on" risk almost certain emotional pain, social stigmatization, psychological damage, and possibly physical harm by going to the dark side? "It goes back to the thrill," said one young lady. "It's like

I got him, he's mine, and everyone knows it." "So it's like some kind of competition between women then?" was my comment. "Well, yeah, sort of," said another young woman. She continued by saying, "When you're walking down the street with a bad boy on your arms, everybody notices you."

It is quite obvious that the "everybody" this young lady was referring to was other women. From this it became apparent that a challenge likely has a dual meaning in the minds of women in thug love. First, the craving for the bad boy is satisfied because he is viewed as best being able to provide the excitement and adventure the woman seeks. This is an inward type of satisfaction. But on the other hand, there is an outward kind of satisfaction that the woman experiences in that being seen with a bad boy somehow validates her womanhood. For example, some women believe that having the bad boy, the alpha male, on their side will elevate their social status. So, at the end of the day, "a challenge," at least in the context of the Zondra Hughes article, is a woman-versus-woman thing as much as it is a woman-to-man thing. We will see this play out in real time when we discuss the case studies on this topic. The final comment related to the descriptors on "a challenge" comes from the Internet article "Why Good Girls Love Bad Boys" by Lisa Daily, where she states, in part, that

> part of us just like [*sic*] that down-to-our-toes thrill, the excitement of something we KNOW is bad for us. (Like chocolate cheesecake, and Jimmy Choo shoes.) Some of us are just gluttons for misery.

The "gluttons for misery" statement was an absolute head turner. When asked for responses to that part of the comment, nearly everyone in the discussion group—the women, that is—agreed that they fell into that category at various points in their lives. Some indicated that they were currently in this state. At this point, I didn't know if I should even be surprised any more. One young lady said,

"It's like being an alcoholic; you just know you're an alcoholic." The fact that many women admit they are gluttons for misery basically means they are willing to do practically anything, including being miserable, to be accepted by a bad boy. I couldn't manufacture a better description of what women do to keep thug love alive.

Most of us are familiar with the saying "misery likes company." While this is a clever and witty-sounding cliché, the reality is that more often than not, misery is mainly realized or played out when one is alone. This brings us to the inevitable: is the excitement, adventure, and the thrill (mainly sex) of being with the bad boy worth the misery that is bound to result? Unfortunately, it appears that many women would answer yes or at least be willing to put up with some misery. At first, this was most disturbing and difficult to comprehend because women who select thug love for a lifestyle are seemingly always giving up so much and getting so little, if anything, in return. But the chilling truth is that there are women who actually don't want much more than sex. I still found this challenging to decipher until I ran across this comment in an Internet article entitled "Why Good Girls Choose Bad Boys" by Joanne Truner:

> Well, my addiction was men, and not just any men—
> the more tattooed, pierced, and party animal, the better.
> I liked men I knew I could never marry, men you would
> never leave alone with a child (or a parent, for that matter).
> The more outrageously different from me they were, the
> better. I was the proverbial "good girl" attracted to the
> "bad boy."

This is a rather startling statement on any level, but what makes it so captivating is the fact that this woman was transparent enough to say it openly and for public consumption for that matter. In most of the group discussions, women said she was definitely keeping it real. First, she views her attraction to bad boys as an addiction. The majority of those canvassed on this point agreed that thug love can be addictive. Second, we notice from Ms. Truner's comment that she liked men she knew she could never marry. The obvious interpretation here is that she was not interested in or looking for a serious or long-term relationship, and of course, a husband was out of the question. Since so many women in group discussions agreed with the first part of Truner's point about being addicted to bad boys, I wondered how many of them would concur with her about not being interested in a guy she could marry. Not many group participants agreed with her on this point. So what can I reasonably deduct from women admitting they are addicted to bad boys on the one hand but put a thumbs-down on not wanting to have a guy they could marry on the other? A reasonable interpretation is that they enjoy the unpredictability and dangers associated with bad boys and have no problem with this lifestyle, but apparently only for a while. It seems that women who think like this could be called players. Correction: they *should* be called players. In some circles they are referred to as "bad girls." Ms. Truner says she was the "proverbial 'good girl,' looking for a bad boy," but it seems more appropriate that she was a "good girl gone bad."

So what's the bottom line to all that we now know about "a challenge"? What happens when the thrill is over? We now know that thug love excitement and adventure can be hazardous to a woman's health. Let's not forget that "a challenge" encompasses danger and unpredictability, not to mention possible injury or harm. Most importantly, however, that "down-to-the-toes thrill" that Lisa Daily says the bad boy provides is only a temporary fix to what is likely an addiction. So when the bedroom scene is over, is there quality interaction on other interpersonal levels? Better still, how often do you have nonintimate quality quiet time? Can you take him home to your parents? Does he spend more time with his male friends than with you? Research suggests that the answers to these questions are most likely not favorable. So who benefits from "a challenge"? It's obvious that the bad boy benefits the most because almost everything about "a challenge" is short term, and short term is what being a bad boy is all about. There is nothing tangible in a relationship based on thrills, and hence the woman loses because she will in fact become as "temporary" as the thrill. And even if the woman is not looking for anything more than a temporary thrill herself, she still loses because a certain level of her personal dignity will be tarnished in order to function in a relationship that is primarily based on a thrill. And a stained and tainted personal dignity has devastating psychological consequences because it is the most difficult thing to rebuild. Based on this, the risky behavior of "a challenge" turns out to be "the challenge."

Chapter 6

"I Can Fix Him"

First Encounters

Several psychological principles took hold of my attention as I came face to face with the first encounters of the "I can fix him" attraction to bad boys. But among these several principles, it was the nature/nurture phenomenon that stayed on the forefront of my thinking because it seemed to be the most probable root of the "I can fix him" mindset. Some people think of nurturing as taking care of someone or fixing them. In thug love, women seem to view "fixing him" as taking care of someone. Either way it's viewed, the bottom line is that fixing is taking care of and taking care of is fixing. Hence, nurturing is at the core of this behavior. As the discussions on "I can fix him" took place over the years, a vast majority of women usually agreed that this was indeed a reason that they were attracted to bad boys and further agreed that an element of nurturing was definitely present in the woman in the form of a "fixing" or "taking care of him" attitude.

One of the first questions that came to mind about fixing the bad boy was *Fixing him from what to what?* From the two previous thug love attractions, we know that women want their bad boys exciting and thrilling so they definitely would not want to fix them from that. We also know that women are attracted to bad boys for protection so they surely wouldn't want to fix him from providing that perceived need. So the question remains: what then needs to be fixed? As always, the best way to approach this attraction, as with the other attractions, is to examine the mindset behind this motivation.

First of all, the "I can fix him" mindset seems to be one in which the woman is seeking a sense of purpose in her own life. And she sees the fulfillment of this need being realized through nurturing, taking care of someone. The idea that this is embedded in a sense of purpose is amplified by Rob Eager, who also maintains that there is a link between purpose and nurturing in his Internet article "Why Do Good Girls Date Bad Boys?" In making this point, he asserts:

> Some women allow their "nurturing instinct" to affect whom they choose to date. In other words, a nice girl may view a bad boy as a "project" or someone whom she can help "fix." This incident occurs when a woman acknowledges that her boyfriend has character flaws, yet believes she can help him mature or overcome his problems. Helping a man to "grow up" can play into a woman's sense of significance.

According to Eager, the nurturing instinct is such a dominant instinct that it is often a factor in the selection process of whom women choose to interact with personally. Thus, the nurturing instinct is a type of feeler that goes out in search of a man—in this case, a bad boy. Of course, in their mind, this is exactly the type of guy who they deem is in need of fixing. Eager refers to this as "a project" or someone the woman, in her mindset, can fix. In order for the fix to materialize, she must be fully in control. As we expand on this view, it becomes apparent that the "I can fix him" mentality is more about self in that it helps the woman assert or reaffirm her own importance or self-worth. Controlling a situation or a person is a good way to accomplish this need. With this controlling mindset, what the woman is trying to fix is what she perceives are character flaws.

While the nature of the character flaws are not pointed out by Eager in his commentary, we know from studying thug love what some of the character flaws of the bad boy are likely to be. From the profile data, a couple of typical character flaws are that the bad boy is likely to be selfish or that his respect for women is very low, if any at all. Whatever the case may be, women who attempt to fix the character failings of bad boys are basically fighting a losing battle. It is highly improbable the "project" will be successful, which means the sense of purpose they seek will not be realized. The almost certain failure will ultimately have a boomerang effect and return to the women in the form of low self-esteem or self-worth.

The second mindset behind the "I can fix him" attempt stems from a past experience or experiences of abuse or neglect from the woman's father. Consider what Rob Eager writes in this regard:

> If a woman was abused or ignored by her father, she may not know how to identify character or real love. Worse, she may subconsciously think that her past pain can be erased by marrying a bad boy and making everything work out right. The fallacy of this belief is that it's impossible to make a man improve his character. He may fake integrity over the short term, but a man will only mature when he makes the decision himself.

In this depiction, the father-daughter relationship is the most significant dynamic. The relationship, or the lack thereof, between a father and a daughter plays a huge role in many of the future interpersonal relationships of women. As we see from this scenario, the abuse or neglect of a father to his daughter can totally cloud her judgment in recognizing "real love." This is a serious problem because thug love thrives on a woman's inability to see through the bad boy's real intentions. Being wronged by Dad not only clouds her judgment but also creates in her a desire to find a way to remove or compensate for the pain and discomfort experienced by the abuse and neglect. In an attempt to remedy this issue, the woman often seeks out someone who she feels she can fix or improve, which in her mindset will eradicate the pains of the past. Keep in mind that some of this is played out in the subconscious which often tries to sort out past traumatic events. This accounts, in part, for the risky behavior that ultimately manifests in the woman's attempts to resolve these issues.

What the woman is trying to fix is twofold. Initially, she seeks a man who she feels needs a character makeover, which is largely what she believes was wrong with Dad. A bad boy really fits this bill. This will put her in a position where everything turns out right as opposed to the wrong that she previously and painfully experienced with Dad. The second part of this is that by making it right, her self-worth increases, giving her a more positive outlook about her life and her future.

Another helpful look into a woman's mindset to "Fix Him" is found in another comment by Lisa Daily from her Internet article "Why Good Girls Love Bad Boys," where she says, "Part of us actually like to believe we can be the one girl to turn this wild man into a pussycat." This is a slightly different attitude than the two previous mindsets. It seems clear that there is an element of competition in this mentality. Who she is competing with is not clear although it is most likely herself. But what is the gain in accomplishing this "pussycat" goal other than the satisfaction of knowing that she was able to change a bad boy to a good boy. The woman who has this mindset is in for a rude awakening. But before I get to that, there is an intriguing inconsistency in wanting to make a bad boy a "pussycat." Simply put, all the qualities of a bad boy that a woman is supposedly attracted to would never be found in a "pussycat." So what gives with this irrational thinking? Perhaps it's the control, the superwoman syndrome, or just plain arrogance. Most likely it's a combination of all the above, but from a researcher's perspective, this further illustrates that there are deep-seated psychological issues associated with the unstable conduct of thug love.

Finally, trying to help improve a person is a noble undertaking, but changing a person is just not going to happen unless the person wants to change. And even if we could change a person, it is highly unlikely it would happen with a bad boy. A student once said that she told her bad boy if he wanted to keep her he had to stop selling drugs. She said he stopped and looked at me with this victorious kind of expression and said, "I changed him." "Really?" I commented. "How do you know this? Are you with him 24/7?" I then asked the group what they thought. Most of them felt that he may have stopped doing it in front of her but didn't believe he gave it up altogether. At that point, I referred her back to a comment that was made by Rob Eager where he said:

> It's impossible to make a man improve his character.
> He may fake integrity over the short term, but a man will
> only mature when he makes the decision himself.

The lesson to this young lady, and all such young ladies who feel they can or even have changed a man, is that no change ever occurs until the person makes the decision to do so themselves. We can nudge him along, but he still has to do the work for and by himself. If you still have a problem accepting this as a fact of life, just ask any recovering alcoholic or drug addict. It turns out that the young lady who said that she did change her boyfriend found out that he was indeed still dealing drugs behind her back.

An in-depth and profound light has been shed with the first encounters of the three reasons women are attracted to bad boys. The surveys have provided an abundance of rich profile information while the many small- and large-group discussions have yielded painstaking but far-reaching intelligence on this topic. But there is still more work to do to secure the most reliable and valid information of this human attraction. To facilitate this, we now turn our attention to case studies as they take us behind the scenes where we see the reliability and validity of the surveys and the group discussions on the three main reasons women are attracted to bad boys.

CHAPTER 7

Case Studies

Making the case with case studies is a researcher's dream, a bad boy's nightmare, and a woman's awakening. To the researcher, the dream of helping women in thug love with reliable, life-changing information becomes a reality through the power of case studies. To the bad boys, the nightmare of losing the control they have over their women eventually becomes a reality through the uncovering and revealing nature of case studies. And to the women in thug love, case studies have transformational qualities—the kind that will help make significant inroads to changing risky behavior into responsible behavior. This is just what the doctor ordered. But it's a little too early to claim healing just yet. Medicine that often cures us is not usually effective unless it is taken as prescribed, with an understanding of how and why it works as well as the side effects. The same holds true for case studies. Understanding how and why the bad boy case studies work not only promotes its effectiveness but also provides the bases for the interventions and strategies to redirect this precarious behavior—not to mention how these strategies can be maintained even if there are adverse side effects.

Like going from analog to high definition, case studies give a much more crystallized and in-depth view. They let one clearly see things about a person that were either not noticed before or were hidden from plain view. Of course, the bad boy prefers it this way—keeping more revealing things about himself unnoticed or hidden from view because his success largely depends on his ability to operate in what is essentially an undercover manner. I like to refer to it as operating in stealth mode or, at a minimum, on a need-to-know basis. But the high-definition view that case studies provide in a phenomenon such as thug love is priceless. Let me explain it this way: A car going over the medium strip on a two-lane road headed straight toward you can be a very sobering sight. With the clarity of a high-definition view, you notice that the driver is distracted by what appears to be some type of cell phone use, most likely texting. What you originally viewed as a potentially dangerous situation is now seen as possibly imminent. The odds of a person recovering from such a distraction in time is not good. But with the help of a high-definition view, you have the time—albeit only seconds at best—to avert this dangerous situation. This is exactly the effect that case studies have on thug love. As it becomes clear to the woman that her relationship with her bad boy will almost certainly evolve from being potentially dangerous to being imminently dangerous, the high-definition view provides just enough time to avoid a possible disaster. Because of this nearly certain outcome, it is imperative that we examine case studies from an overview perspective first. Doing so, before looking at the actual recounts of the lived experiences, provides the proper insight to effectively analyze its impact. This prevents creating a false reality and gets one closer to the help that will bring about change.

Now that we know what case studies do, understanding how it makes its mark is just as important a component to mapping out a recovery plan. The up-front, close, and personal nature of case studies is just that—personal. And the personal aspect of case studies is the main "how" ingredient. There are several characteristics of these personal accounts that provide the construction material to build and map out an effective escape route out of thug love.

To begin with, personal accounts consist of firsthand information. Since there is no hearsay, gossip, or speculation in firsthand accounts, it can have the same force as in the courtroom—it can convict the charged, in this case the bad boy. Second, because there is nearly always a high-definition quality in personal accounts, they produce a clear and concise picture. It's the kind of detailed information necessary to prevent any major flaws in the recovery plan. This is important because, let's face it, it's easy to overlook and not see something important when emotions are involved. When the high-stake emotions of thug love are in the mix, women will oftentimes willingly overlook or just plain refuse to see certain things, especially unflattering things about someone with whom they are having an interpersonal relationship. But with the high-definition view, the details cannot be easily discounted or played down because the sharpness of such a picture is easily imprinted into the mind and is therefore constantly in your face and just won't go away.

Furthermore, the personal view provided through case studies almost always contains educating value. One of the bad boy's greatest fears is his woman—or should I say *women*—becoming knowledgeable in his ways. Make no mistake, bad boys do not get to be successful by being naïve and unschooled at what they do. They are keenly aware that a well-informed woman will blow up their game, leaving them ineffective, null and void, and, hopefully from our point of view, alone.

Finally, and perhaps most importantly, the personal accounts of our bad boy case studies disclose patterns of behavior that all but seals the deal in providing the final instructions for the recovery plan. Patterns of behavior are extremely powerful tools in helping people discern and correct problematic conduct. They can have that "breaking news, this just in" effect. When they surface, as they did while investigating this lifestyle, patterns have the kind of stuff that often helps solve some of those "whodunit" movies or perhaps one of those crime-style mystery novels. In thug love, this is especially significant because whodunit is not always that obvious. Patterns are also the kind of stuff that verifies the extent of a phenomenon. In thug love, we found that there are bad boys all over the world as the personal accounts in case studies include women internationally. And this provides a sense of bonding because so many women can relate to the stories of others to such an extent that they can predict the play before the player makes his move, something like a quarterback reading the defense and realizes a blitz is coming. And, finally, these patterns serve as reminders that the women are not alone, that their cause does not sit on some isolated island, out of sight, out of mind.

Approximately forty case studies were conducted, mostly during the last three years of this seven-plus–year investigation. Included were approximately eighteen Caucasian women, fourteen African American women, two Hispanic women, two mixed women, one Native American woman, two African women, a woman with a Middle Eastern background, and a woman from the LGBT community. A little over half of these interviews were used in making this definitive case about thug love, mainly because after hearing anywhere from five to six of the recounts of each of the three attractions, they began to repeat themselves. Since no new information surfaced, it served no purpose to include every single "lived experience." All of the women volunteered to be interviewed and agreed to have their interview recorded with the assurance that the highest degree of confidentiality would be applied to their recorded accounts. To ensure that their privacy was maintained, all the names have been changed. An interesting footnote here is that at least five of these women said that they didn't mind if I used their real names. Of course, I turned down their offer, but I found this was most revealing as one could reasonably determine from such an offer that these women might have been trying to get back at their bad boys. The majority of the case studies were from college-educated women. Around 40 percent of these were in undergraduate school seeking bachelor degrees while another 40 percent were women pursuing master's degrees. The majority of the college women were also working women. The remaining 20 percent of the interviewees were women who only worked. They included professional women from the private and public sectors, young women just entering the job market, and a few women who owned businesses. The age range was from seventeen to fifty. It should also be noted here that even to this day, women are still volunteering to tell their bad boy stories.

These fearless young ladies have basically put the most powerful exclamation point on the bad boy phenomenon—they put a face on this perpetrator. Their courage must be noted and celebrated because rehashing stories of personal failures and mistreatment can be an emotionally draining endeavor. This became noticeable when some of the interviews would almost seem like therapy sessions. Even so, these valuable reflections were no longer a matter of just data and theories but rather reflected the actual real-time human experiences of women in thug love.

CHAPTER 8

"Protection" Case Studies

> I lost myself in the relationship because in order to secure the protection I needed I had to cater to him—his needs, desires, etc. Also, in order to be protected I had to basically give up my family.

Protection = control = protection. There is just no other way to put it. In thug love, you won't find one without the other. The opening comment from the "lived experiences" of Natalie not only corroborates this triangular paradigm but in doing so also reveals the complex nature and twisted thinking of women who are attracted to bad boys for "protection." The thinking is twisted because at the end of the day, *protection* is merely a code word for control, and the willingness to be controlled is linked to the need to be needed, and the need to be needed can only be accomplished through being protected. Not only do the narratives of this attraction confirm the link between protection and control, but even more astonishing, the recounts also raised serious doubts as to whether any real protection even occurred in the first place. And if by chance some level of protection did seem to take place, it ultimately worked only for the benefit of the bad boy, not of the woman.

The price of protection is very high, and control is the only payment that will be accepted by the bad boys. Natalie was well aware of this. In her opening statement at the beginning of this chapter, Natalie paid the price and made the control payment when she reflected, "In order to be protected I had to basically give up my family." Again, the only way this can be accomplished by the bad boy is through controlling his woman. Natalie was a white woman in her late twenties and was one of the first young ladies to volunteer to share her personal accounts regarding protection and bad boys. She was very thoughtful and deliberate as she recounted her experiences. Natalie is a good example of how this twisted thinking looks in real life. When I raised the notion that through my research I have found that *protection* is another code word for control, she responded, "Oh, yeah! Tell me about it. I'm always in control. I still am always in control of everything." When asked whether he tried to control her, she replied, "Yeah! I lost a lot of my family for a long time." The false reality that Natalie created, or better still was created for her, had blinded her to the reality that losing her family was in fact a matter of control over her. Where there are false realities, there is twisted thinking. Also, Natalie never mentioned anything that her bad boy gave up for her, yet she believed that she was in control. At any rate, it was clear she was either in serious denial that he was in control of her or she has been under his control for so long it is no longer viewed as such.

Inwardly, many women know they are being controlled, but outwardly, most are usually in denial. It is imperative to confront and remove this psychological defense mechanism because it provides a crutch for women to lean on—allowing the denial to play the role of an enabler to the control. And if denial is allowed to remain unchallenged, it will certainly impede any effort to arrest and replace the unsafe behavior associated with the protection attraction. Perhaps another way to express it is that a person can't change a behavior that they don't believe exists. The fact is that the link between protection and control is practically unbreakable. Crystallizing this fact helps remove the denial because it removes the crutch. An excellent illustration of the unbreakable relationship between protection and control involves the president of the United States. There are few who would argue that the president is definitely one of the most, if not the most, protected men in the world. In order for his protection to occur with effectiveness and efficiency, the Secret Service has to control him—perhaps not in a literal sense but definitely in a tactical sense—by controlling his movements, his flow, and in some cases how long he stays in one location. And even if the protection and control does not impact where he goes, it certainly impacts how he goes where he goes. I think the connection between protection and control has been well established at this point. Of course, the type of protection that women want with their bad boys is not even remotely close to the level of protection that the president receives; however, the concept and the process is basically the same.

Candice essentially cosigned on Natalie's experiences and also introduced a new component of this attraction. A very serious-minded African American woman, Candice in her early twenties was animated and forceful in telling her story. She was reasonably transparent considering the nature of what she was sharing. However, it was easy to tell from her body language that the pain was still fresh in her mind as though it happened yesterday:

> He really didn't protect me but he controlled me for a while. My mom didn't like him. She knew about him. She just happened to be snooping around and found out he had a couple of charges on him. I found out that if I wanted to be with him and have his protection then I would have to be under his control. He would verbally express that he didn't want me to go out with friends. I would agree with this most of the time.

Notice that both Candice and Natalie knew they would have to be under their bad boys' control to get protection. Two women, from two different walks of life, not to mention almost ten years apart in age, were basically saying the exact same thing. To be clear, they recognized and admitted that control was involved. A coincidence? I think not! In fact, from the many group discussions held on this topic, quite a few women shared similar stories of being controlled to get protection from their bad boy. Even case studies from the attraction of "a challenge" and "I can fix him" contained stories of protection and control as a secondary reason. But it was Candice's declaration that *he really didn't protect me* that was eye-opening. Amazing! Not only has being controlled been consciously repressed, we now find out that the protection which is sought from the bad boy often never materializes as well.

Keisha joins her female colleagues on the protection attraction and also confirms Candice's revelation that real protection in a bad boy relationship is rare at best:

> And I think the reason that I liked it the most was, like, the protection part of it because at times, like, when going out with him I would say, "Well I don't have to worry about anybody messing with me." I was, like, you know, I felt safe when I really wasn't, but I felt like I was.

Keisha, a nineteen-year-old African American lady, presented as being a little feisty, at least on the outside. But as her narrative went forward, it became apparent that she was a much more complicated person. If we just take her comment that "I felt safe when I really wasn't, but I felt like I was," it seems clear that she is a confused individual when it comes to her bad boy affairs. A major contributor to Keisha's confused state of mind is most likely being involved in unstable social arrangements. Nonetheless, validating Candice's disclosure that real protection is scarce can be very helpful to other women in similar situations. Keisha originally interviewed as an "I can fix him" attraction, but her story seemed a little more suitable for the protection attraction.

The logical and reasonable question at this point is why would women forsake their families and friends for what they feel is protection from a bad boy, especially when the possibilities of acquiring such security is little to none. To obtain dependable answers, we must first notice that in each of the three case studies above, it was either explicit or implied that the woman had to give up something very important—family and friends—to maintain a relationship with her bad boy. This is control over movement. To gain this much power over a person, it only seems reasonable that the bad boy had to at least first demonstrate some ability to protect the woman. Some women indicated their bad boys were very muscular while others such as Georgia went so far as to say, "I married someone who knew how to shoot and kill people. So the protection thing was definitely on top of my mind." Whatever it consisted of, the case studies reveal that the women totally bought into it. Making such serious demands on women, such as where they can go and whom they can see, is clearly an ego issue on the part of the bad boy. And the fact that he needs to have his ego pumped up suggests his own weaknesses in this area. The question is why somebody who bills himself as a bad boy would need a daily ego boost.

Second, women must be held accountable for their actions in thug love. This is not only about the bad boy. So what role does the woman play in allowing herself to be caught up in such an unrealistic attraction? The short answer is putting their behavior before their thinking. On this side of the dynamic, a clear and concise definition of what protection consists of is not really understood among many women. In most lived experiences, protection was based on something that "might" or "might not" happen—like a bar room brawl, a fight at a party, or some guy trying to hit on the woman. Outside of a woman getting hit on, how many times do you think something like this is going to happen, and, even more importantly, what kind of places do women go where this behavior is acted out on a regular basis? By the way, no one who shared their protection stories indicated ever experiencing any of these events. To further illustrate this point, let's remember what Candice said: "He really didn't protect me, but controlled me for a while." If he didn't protect her, it was most likely because there was no compelling reason to do so. Therefore, part of this protection attraction in many women's mindsets is basically a "just in case" situation. When Natalie was asked whether her bad boy provided something that she needed in the way of protection, she said, "I wanted to be there." When asked what for, she replied, "Just be there! Just be there!" I asked, "Is that all you needed?" She said, "Uh-hum." These case studies and similar information from group discussions point more to a need-to-be-needed attitude than just a need-to-be-protected mindset. Somehow the two intersected quite frequently in these women's thinking, with the need-to-be-needed mindset often being the frontrunner.

Thirdly, and this is by no means in order of importance, protection can be viewed as a referendum on "Dad." We will see in the research of thug love that throughout all of these case studies, Dad plays a major role in the mindset of women with respect to why they are attracted to bad boys. In any event, there seems to be a link between dads and their daughters' attraction to bad boys for protection. Let's take a look at a few excerpts of case studies in this regard:

> GEORGIA: I needed structure. I went out clubbing a lot, two and three times a week. Meeting guys and partying all the time, not respecting my parents. I treated my dad really bad. That's the thing I really regret.

> MARY: At seventeen, I was on my own. My dad just lost it, my mom and dad just didn't have the greatest relationship. He just lost it one day, and we were basically just out on our own.

NATALIE: When I met my husband my dad was real sick with cancer and I needed a distraction.

Insomuch as all three of these women having an issue with their dads, either through abandonment, illness, or just plain insubordination, it appears the protection these women sought was a type of replacement from what they really wanted, needed, or even rejected from their biological dad. Georgia rejected her dad's protection which seems to be in the form of structure to her. The protection she was seeking from her bad boy was an effort to make up for treating her dad badly. Natalie's dad could no longer provide that fatherly protection due to illness; therefore, she looked for it elsewhere. And Mary was looking for protection mainly to rescue herself from having to deal with abandonment issues.

As we mentioned earlier, protection is an excellent reinforcement for the bad guy's ego. But women, even though being controlled most of the time, seem to try to find a way to rationalize some benefit from their thug love arrangement. Let's call it a little fantasy self-worth buildup or workout—although at the expense of being in a nearly jail-like relationship. Nevertheless, listen to a few of the question-and-answer interactions of some of the case studies in this regard:

QUESTION: What kind of guys do you like?

LAURA: Gangsters!

QUESTION: What's your turn on to that?

LAURA: They aren't afraid of getting in trouble. If they have, like, anger problems and they're not afraid to fight, then they can like stand up for you and *protect* you.

QUESTION: So you need somebody to take care of you.

GEORGIA: Like, yeah, take up for me too. That's the main thing, I guess, take up.

QUESTION: You can't take up for yourself?

GEORGIA: Well, I can, but.

QUESTION: But you prefer somebody else to do it?

GEORGIA: I think it's attractive that the guy you are with will take up for you.

QUESTION: But your protection is more about security?

MARY: Security, yeah because I was spending for myself at a very early age. And I was thinking, well, you know two incomes have to be better than one. Having someone to talk to and don't have to work, you know, three or four jobs and anyway it didn't work out because, like, I became pregnant right after we got married and he was real controlling and didn't want me to work.

Notice that whether it was viewed as "attractive," "a turn on," or "security," the common underlying theme with these women was self-worth. The protection that these women coveted was, bottom line, intended to build, reinforce, or massage their self-worth. Laura originally interviewed as "a challenge" attraction but had a compelling level of the protection attraction in her experience. Therefore, she was the only one who made the more-than-one—attraction list. A slim and sort of cagey twenty-year-old white woman, Laura told her story with great articulation and seemed to enjoy doing so. At times during her interview, she seemed to be getting something off of her chest.

In the excerpt from her case study above, she believed that if her man stood up for her, then that meant that she was worth something important enough to fight for even if that came with the price of being controlled. In Georgia's case, she first admits that she needed somebody to take care of her, but more telling is the phrase "take up for me too." This "me too" suggests that Georgia is saying, "I want to know that I count also." In other words, she needed a self-worth, self-image boost as well. Georgia was a twenty-four-year-old Caucasian graduate student who reported several encounters with bad boys and was very careful in sharing the details of her experiences. And finally, Mary, a stately Caucasian woman in her late forties was the only interviewee whose protection attraction was for that physical security. Mary was vigorous and aggressive in volunteering to tell her story and was very meticulous and detailed in the process. The security she sought provided her with a sense of self-worth that came from the comfort of knowing or believing that she was important enough to a man to put such things as a roof over her head. Of course, it is important to note here that Mary is one of the older case study volunteers, and as such, her protection recounts involved more history than most and therefore was a little more concrete than abstract.

From our case studies we know that protection comes with a price. A warning to women under the bad boy "protection" plan—it often leads to violence and abuse, physical or otherwise, heavy drug use or dealing, and generally being involved in an unhealthy environment that looks like anything but "protection" being provided. Now don't get me wrong: violence, drugs, and abuse were rampant in all three of the attraction reasons, but the protection reason was most baffling because it basically resulted in the exact opposite of what the women said they wanted. They sought protection but often received danger instead. Perhaps a few patterns from the case studies will better make the point.

Jenny, a twenty-eight-year-old Caucasian woman, was very poised and graceful but, like Georgia, seemed to choose her words very carefully in her interview. She said, "He was into drugs and had to go to rehab." She would later indicate that when she met her bad boy, he was in the military and liked breaking the rules. This is where Jenny's earlier statement is worth repeating: "I married someone who knew how to shoot and kill people. So the protection thing was definitely on top of my mind." While Jenny didn't mention any physical abuse, there were clear signs that psychological abuse was no stranger in their relationship when she stated, "I mean, he liked to push people's buttons. He would try to see how far he could get you to go, to see how you would react." When pressed for an explanation as to the attractiveness of this behavior, Jenny was somewhat reluctant to discuss it but eventually said, "I don't know. I really don't know. I don't know, maybe it was, it was he was just different. I guess at the time I was just looking for something different. I've always liked guys that were a little different, a little off" (she began laughing). If there ever was clear evidence of inviting trouble at the very start of a relationship, here it is.

Mary indicated that her protection was mainly for security, but even this came with a price, a violent price, although she refused to acknowledge it at first. When asked if there was any physical abuse in the relationship, Mary responded, "Physically, he never hit me, but he would throw me into things." Not only is this clear rationalizing and/or just plain denial; she also clearly demonstrated the ability to push things into her unconsciousness when she said, "Yeah. Um, one time he threw me down on the couch and spit in my face and I don't really remember what I had done for that. Sometimes stuff just didn't seem to matter anymore" (Mary started to tear up). Moving forward, Mary began to feel comfortable enough to just totally unload and shared the story of why she left her bad boy: "He was a heavy drinker, and one evening he got very drunk and for some reason he was angry and went upstairs to get his gun, and I grabbed the kids and ran out of the house and drove to a secure location." So much for protection and control!

The price of protection from a psychological perspective was most informative as well when we observe the fact that Candice considered control itself to be abuse. To this view she eventually said:

> The constant accusations of me being with other guys was the determining factor that led me to leave. He was telling me every day that I was with somebody and it just got to be too much. He was accusing me and it turns out that it was him doing the cheating.

Georgia's price for control was being cheated on. Although through most of the protection women felt that cheating was also going on in their relationships, they had no hard proof. When asked how many times she thought she was cheated on, Georgia said, "Probably twice, I think, well . . . it could have been more." So while Georgia thought she was receiving the protection she desired, along with being controlled and having no social friends, her bad boy was taking advantage of knowing exactly where she was and used this knowledge to cheat on her. I wonder how many women are willing to see the clear picture of what is going on here with respect to this protection phenomenon.

After hearing the various stories and even becoming a part of their experiences through their testimonies, the patterns are most profound as they provide a close-up perspective and enlightenment on this topic. So what have we learned? First, we know that there is an undeniable connection between protection and control. Second, there is a pattern of women giving up something to obtain this so-called protection, usually family and friends. Third, the relationship between daughter and dad plays a major role in the mindset that develops the need for protection. Fourth is that a pattern is established in which a false sense of self-worth is adopted. And fifth, there are definite patterns of violence, physical abuse, and drug abuse, as well as various degrees of psychological abuse associated with protection.

With the exception of Laura and Keisha, Jenny, Candice, Natalie, Georgia, and Mary all married their "protection" men and they would all eventually get divorced. The protection phenomenon was the only one where this married/divorce pattern was present. And this pattern, along with all the other patterns of behavior that surfaced in this attraction, makes a powerful statement. The fact that seven different women would all have so much in common simply highlights the far-reaching impact of thug love in today's social world. And although the protection attraction ultimately fails women, the commonalities found among these young ladies can be very useful in developing strategies to reject this reason for being attracted to bad boys.

CHAPTER 9

"A Challenge" Case Studies

Adventure! Exciting! Dangerous! Unpredictable! Sounds like descriptions of a roller-coaster ride or perhaps the words of someone who had just taken a bungee jump. Even though we met these terms in the first encounters of this attraction, some may still find it difficult to fully comprehend that these are descriptions routinely used by women to express why they were attracted to bad boys for "a challenge." And by the time their stories were told, these women did indeed end up experiencing roller-coaster–like rides in their relationships and in most cases ended up with more than they bargained for. Now work with me for just a minute: a little adventure and perhaps some excitement could be a welcomed and sometimes needed component in a relationship. In measured and reasonable moderation, it could possibly help stimulate, sustain, and even enhance a relationship. But "dangerous" and "unpredictable" take this "a challenge" phenomenon to a whole new level—a level which rises not only to erratic and volatile relationships but also, even worse, to relationships where the erratic is physical and psychological abuse and the volatile is drug and alcohol misuse. In spite of this, these types of challenges remain steadfast with women even though most

---

of them know that their risky behavior will almost certainly involve serious consequences. And the type of consequences involved are the kind which are most difficult, if not almost impossible to recover from, leaving many of these women with what basically comes close to social death sentences.

From an investigative perspective, the mindset of craving adventure, excitement, danger, and unpredictability in relationships seems cavalier, and brazen, and of course, irresponsible. But these are peripheral descriptors, the kind that are often used to cover up or mask what is really behind this questionable mentality. Uncovering the origins of this conduct will point us to a cause, a trigger, and a pretext. And the degree with which we comprehend the genesis of this behavior is usually the degree with which we are able to develop effective strategies to change for the better. The descriptors used in this attraction point to some serious underlining psychological issues which could easily be described as inner battles. The case studies bear this out as the roller-coaster ride of the "a challenge" attraction comes alive in the forms of cheating, physical abuse, drugs, and much more—all brought on by what seems to be the out-of-control desire for "a challenge."

Laura, a slender twenty-year-old white woman, whom we first met in the protection case study, was anxious to tell her story. This was evident in the fact that she contacted me several times to remind me of the interview appointment. The recounting of her bad boy experiences seemed to be therapeutic. When Laura was asked what "a challenge" meant to her, she responded:

> Like if you know that he's bad, a bad boy who likes
> multiple girls at once, you want that challenge to have him
> be yours only.

In Laura's case, the adventure was in knowing the bad boy had multiple girls while the excitement was the challenge of trying to make the bad boy "yours only." The unpredictability is demonstrated in Laura's response to a follow-up question: "How do you know if you've done it [made him 'yours only']?" Here, she openly admitted that "you don't know." Her compulsive desire for experiencing danger in her bad boy relationships was manifested in two ways. First, Laura described her bad boy as being a "gangster" wherein she admitted that such a dangerous lifestyle turned her on. This is because in her mind, this meant that he would fight for her. On the other hand, she also felt that his dangerous lifestyle was a challenge for her to change him. At this point in the interview, it became obvious that Laura could be a candidate for the "I can fix him" attraction as well. However, she fell just short of making it a triple hitter. Nevertheless, when asked, "Change him from what to what?" Laura replied, "Um, being a cheater and from doing drugs." Second, when asked if he ever hit her, Laura replied, "Not hit, but pushed me. He always, like, left bruises on my arms. He would grab my arms, and he would, like, shake me." Unless Laura in some sort of way felt that bruises and being pushed were not considered mistreatment, it appears that the need for excitement, adventure, and unpredictability blinded her from the reality of recognizing the clear and present signs of abuse. Since we are on this topic at the moment, it is imperative that I emphasize the fact that there are quite a few women who view mild abuse (if there is such a thing) as a guy showing how much he cares about you. If nothing else is resolved as a result of this thug love research, this particular mindset *must* be changed. There is far too much physical and psychological abuse in interpersonal relationships in our society that has either been unconsciously repressed or consciously swept under the rug. And this pertains to all types of relationships, not just thug love. On second thought, if you are in any kind of interpersonal relationship where physical or psychological abuse is occurring, IT IS THUG LOVE!

Melissa was a neatly dressed and well-groomed Caucasian young lady in her midtwenties. She described herself as "not attractive, just average," and while somewhat guarded and cautious at the outset of sharing her story, she eventually opened up:

The challenge was not that "I can fix him" but rather "I can get him." It was kind of like leading a double life. I knew that he was telling me things that I wanted to hear and it was like a comforting thing to me . . . for somebody who would tell me that I was beautiful. He told me that he was going to buy me a house. . . . He didn't have a job. I knew that he wasn't going to buy me a house. I needed, just a body. Yeah, I was lonely and it was fun. I wanted something different. I knew what I was doing. I knew that it was nothing more than sex mostly. He was the opposite of my husband who was a hard worker, he had a good job.

The similarities between Melissa and Laura are not surprising and we haven't even included the remaining case studies on "a challenge." The adventure for Melissa was the idea of leading a double life while the adventure for Laura involved dealing with bad boys who had multiple girls. Both of their views of adventure and excitement rested on making the bad boy their own. Compare their mindsets in this regard: Melissa said, "The challenge was not that 'I can fix him' but rather 'I can get him'" while Laura said, "You want that challenge [excitement] to have him be yours only." As far as unpredictability is concerned, the fact that Melissa's bad boy didn't have a job made the unpredictability of the relationship a sure thing. But in Laura's case, the unpredictability in her bad boy relationship was a certainty because she was drawn to *a bad boy who likes multiple girls at once.* Any relationship where multiple girls are involved is unpredictable by definition. The danger that both women desired and experienced in their "a challenge" attraction naturally involved dangerous activities. We know that Laura's gravitation to danger ended up with her being around drugs daily as well as being abused. And from her interview, we learned that Melissa's appetite for excitement and danger played a role in her having sexual relations with over 20 men. That's correct! From her own lips, Melissa recounted, "I slept with over 20 men."

———

We now turn to Maxine, the third case study on the "a challenge" attraction. As an African American woman in her midforties, Maxine had a more extensive history of relationships with bad boys. It seems that the depth of her experiences allowed her to express her story with much freedom and candidness.

> I knew it was a dangerous attraction but I went for it because it was exciting. He was a bit younger, like four years or so younger. After years of being somebody's daughter, somebody's mother, somebody's somebody else, I didn't know if I had it anymore. The ability to draw somebody in, the ability to be attractive, the ability to be desired—all those things that women do. And that gives you power. The power that I had over him was that I had something he wanted, something that drove him crazy, something that other people didn't have.

Again, same story, different twist. At the outset, Maxine acknowledges up front that her actions were dangerous, but in her mind, danger was the excitement that added adventure to the relationship. While being so direct and revealing in her dialogue, Maxine's body language at times was sending out a different message. As the discussion continued, it became clear that even in the midst of what she felt was excitement and adventure, something was still missing. She seemed somewhat aggravated over the fact that she spent so many years being what somebody else wanted her to be. But it was equally clear that she now wanted to be liberated, to be who she wanted to be. This was a good sign. Unfortunately, Maxine picked the wrong approach to realizing her goals. First, being liberated seems to be the driving force behind Maxine's concern and subsequent actions about whether she still had it or not: "I didn't know if I had it anymore." There is little doubt that "had it any more" refers to being able to attract men. The problem here is that this is a shallow reason to engage in a relationship. This behavior only serves to massage the ego and does nothing to build and sustain the relationship—it's all about the woman. The evidence of a pattern in this behavior can be found in the fact that this same concern is found in Melissa's outlook: "The challenge was not that 'I can fix him' but rather 'I can get him.'" And not to be outdone, Laura's comment about the bad boy "being yours only" has touches of this same, almost obsessive attitude about being seen by men as being attractive.

Being attractive is a major deal with women regardless of whether they deal with bad boys or not—I really should say a major, major deal, which often borders on obsession. Of course, in all fairness, men are also deeply concerned about whether they still have it or not, but it doesn't appear to be at the level of most women. Nonetheless, we see that Maxine, Melissa, and Laura's attractiveness is at the forefront of their mindset.

Second, being liberated appears to promote Maxine's craving of danger and unpredictability in her relationships. The problem with this approach is that while it didn't lead to physical or drug abuse as in the case of Laura, it did involve psychological abuse which was almost, if not more, traumatic. This became evident when she admitted that sex with her bad boy "was like a drug." Maxine soon found out what unpredictability really looked like when she recounted waking up one morning with her bad boy lying next to her, and he announced that he was going to get married to another woman. Talk about unpredictable! The dangers of dealing with this bad boy became so out of control that she once referred to him as being narcissistic.

Terry was the fourth case study on "a challenge." A Caucasian woman in her early twenties, Terry was the gutsiest of all of the interviewees. Some would probably say she was "All the way live!" She was very eager to tell her story and, in doing so, was direct, to the point, and very thorough in the process. It was my conversation with Terry that helped confirm that not only do a lot of women think alike when it comes to interpersonal relationships, but they behave so much alike as well. Just listen to an excerpt of Terry's opening statement regarding why she likes dealing with bad boys for "a challenge," and even hardcore doubters will begin to realize that there is something very unique, very uniform among women and their thinking as it relates to interpersonal relationships:

> He was actually dating another girl at the time and, like, I have a thing with control. And so, not so much like having to control every situation but, like, if I see something and, like, I kind of want it, like, I will go for it. And I mean, I knew he was bad, you know what I mean, but he was like, he was that guy that all the girls wanted, and, like, he could get any girl that he wanted, you know what I mean. But, like, if he picked you to be his girlfriend that was like, it was like a big deal.

There is absolutely no need for a comparative analysis here because after reading the previous excerpts of Laura's, Melissa's, and Maxine's interviews, this excerpt from Terry is the comparative analysis within itself. It could easily be said: if you read one, you have read them all. While they may not be practically identical in language, they are definitely identical in attitude and mentality. Like all of the ladies before her, Terry found her adventure and excitement in trying to take a guy from another woman: "He was actually dating another girl at the time . . . but, like, if I see something and, like, I kind of want it, like, I will go for it." There is certainly excitement in the prospect of going for it, especially when it involves trying to take another woman's man. With respect to the danger and unpredictability that Terry sought, it was not only present, but it also became a significant part of their daily lives. She recounts that

> he sold drugs, that's how he made his money. He would give me my fix . . . and then it spiraled out of control as the drugs were every part of it but he started hitting me and, like, he would kick me out, like, until I would pass

out. And I would come back to and he'd expect everything to be calm.

The fifth case study for "a challenge" was Maria, a thirty-five-year-old, very religious woman and a native of South America. When she moved to the United States, she said that she started dating guys because she didn't want to be alone. Maria was plainly engaging, so much so that her interview included three sessions. When asked about her attraction to bad boys for "a challenge," she didn't stray far from the rest of her female colleagues even though she grew up thousands of miles away:

> He was definitely a challenge because you would never know how to get him. You would never know what to do to convince him that you were the one for him. All the women wanted him. Women like that because if you get him, it means that you supposedly are better than them. And that's just a stupid challenge that I should have never done.

Maria and her bad boy eventually had two children together. Even though she didn't say specifically she wanted danger and unpredictability, she got a decent dose of it:

> Then I found out that he was doing drugs. Then I found out that he was cheating. Then the relationship got violent. The violence was physical. He used to choke me and many other things. Police would sometimes get involved. Most of the fights and violence was over cheating.

The most heart-wrenching part of Maria's story was that even with the violence, the choking, cheating, and the police involvement, she remained with her bad boy for several years. Thug love's power over women not only brings about real danger, but we have now seen that it can be an addiction as well. From the psychological perspective, this would routinely be viewed as learned helplessness.

By the time I conducted Makeda's interview, the patterns in the "a challenge" attraction have become convincingly clear. In Makeda's case, the sex was there, the drugs were there, and of course, there was no shortage of the dangerous, living-on-the-edge lifestyle. Still, a few things did stand out with respect to her recount:

> He kind of bossed me around and I liked that. I know he controlled me, but I liked that. Yes, it was exciting, it was exciting with him. One day he showed up at my house uninvited with his boys and he wanted to sell his drugs from my house. I was kind of upset about that. I found out that he had been in jail several times and was out on parole. He's now back in jail, but this time it's for murder.

Makeda was an African from Ethiopia. She was twenty-three years old, in graduate school majoring in business administration and the sixth case study on "a challenge." She was very upbeat and seemed to be a little curious about the interview process. She also presented as being somewhat naïve at times. It is important to note that Makeda openly admitted being controlled and bossed around, not to mention that she used one of the challenge descriptors "exciting" to describe how she felt about being treated in this manner.

Yvette, like Maria, lived with her bad boy. A young woman in her early twenties, Yvette had a strong Middle Eastern background. Her mom passed away early in her life, and she didn't know anything about her dad. She did say that she was curious about who her father was. When asked what kind of guys she liked, she commented:

> The ones that were popular. The ones that you feel like you could never get are the ones that I always wanted though.

Yvette shared that she had at least three bad boy relationships. The pattern of drugs, alcohol, and sex would not be broken in her case as well. In fact, she recounts that she was borderline addicted to sex, and when asked if she felt her culture dealt with bad boys differently from American culture, she said:

> Not really. I have three friends from my country living here and we all like bad boys. The drugs, alcohol, and sex is no different. [I]got into trouble with the law as a result of my relationship with a bad boy. This was clearly a case of being in the wrong place with the wrong person.

When asked what the driving force behind her high sex drive was, Yvette responded, "I wanted to do a new experience, wanted to make the other person like me, wanted them to come back for more because I didn't feel good about myself."

Sarah, a very bright young lady in her midtwenties, was the eighth and final case study on the "a challenge" attraction. A Caucasian woman who seemed to describe her bad boy experiences in a cerebral manner, Sarah started off in a different direction but ended up on the same street:

> I broke up with him because he started getting kind of boring. Like he started getting nice. He started to like me and that freaks me out.

Sarah did a reversal of sorts in her bad boy details because she wasn't looking for excitement and danger in her relationship; she was already experiencing it. But when the thrills began to wane, she wanted out. She didn't want any part of a connection with a guy that was remotely normal. And just like all of the "a challenge" case studies, Sarah's bad boy was heavily into the drug scene:

He was really, like, hardcore into drugs—a lot of pills
mainly, um, and he would just kind of like sneak around.
He had all of these interesting stories, like these thrilling
stories. . . . Like he told me this one time how he got high
and had to run from the cops.

When I asked Sarah what the attraction was with such a guy,
she said:

It just got me interested. Not even sexually interested,
just mentally interested. Everything for me is like a mind
game. I don't know why. I just really like the complexity
of stuff like that.

So what could possibly be the genesis of this "a challenge"
attraction? What is behind or what reinforces such hazardous
behavior in women? For starters, there is definitely a "competitive"
mindset involved. This pattern is very strong. Maria saw it as a
battle with other women when she stated, "All the women wanted
him. Women like that because if you get him it means that you
are supposedly better than them." It seemed like Terry lived in the
same neighborhood as Maria as she recalled, "But he was like, he
was that guy that all the girls wanted. . . . but, like, if he picked you
to be his girlfriend, that was, like, it was like a big deal." Maxine's
competitive mindset was comparable when she said, "The ability to
draw somebody in, the ability to be attractive, the ability to be desired,
all those things that women do. And that gives you power." Yvette's
competitive drive was consistent with the pattern when she admitted
that her choice of a bad boy was "the ones that were popular." Of
course, we can't forget that Melissa said, "The challenge was not that
I can change him but that I could get him. And notwithstanding this,
Laura's competitive streak is obvious when she speaks of her bad boy
having "multiple girls" followed by her goal of making him "yours
only." All of these are a stark reminder that women competing with

other women for a man's attention and affection is at the core of the "a challenge" attraction and probably a major reason behind non–thug love relationships as well.

Another mindset behind the challenge behavior is that of power and control. Again, the patterns in the case studies speak for themselves. Maxine would have to be the most obvious of the group when she said, without hesitation, "The power that I had over him was that I had something he wanted." This further exchange with Maxine provided some additional insight regarding the origins of her attitudes on this subject:

> QUESTION: What's so exciting about a challenge?
> MAXINE: Power.
> QUESTION: Power for who?
> MAXINE: For me.
> QUESTION: Why do you need power?
> MAXINE: Because I felt powerless as a kid. My home was a sheltered environment. It was an oppressive environment, not abusive, but oppressive.

Yvette felt she could gain her power by having sex with her bad boys when she said, "[I] wanted them to come back for more because I didn't feel good about myself."

Sarah saw power and control as a mental thing: "Everything for me is like a mind game. I don't know why; I just really like the complexity of stuff like that." Conversely, Makeda seems to part with the pattern here, but only briefly. This is most interesting in that according to her account, she was not looking for power and control but rather enjoyed being controlled. However, she returns to the "a challenge" fold because she still finds this exciting: "He kind of bossed me around, and I like that. I knew he controlled me, but I liked that. Yes, it was exciting, it was exciting with him." The craving or need for power is also evident with Laura, Melissa, and Maria because once again they all recounted in one way or another having the challenge of winning the bad boy over—making him be theirs only. And, of course, the reward of accomplishing this gave them all a sense of power and control. But we know that even if they achieve their goal to win their bad boy, it will only be a temporary arrangement because a challenge begets a challenge," which begets "a challenge," and the cycle will never end until a higher mindset begins.

The case-study view of "a challenge" helps us to understand the cavalier thinking of women who embrace this attraction. These behind-the-scene looks at the "lived experiences" of women who seek a challenge also reveals several common characteristics which can be helpful in understanding this phenomenon: they are free-spirited more often than not, they chose to live on the edge, they are generally not afraid to take risks, their self-worth is in need of repair, and they seem to be responding to some hurt or pain from previous relationships.

The need for power and the need for competition to win is a strong indicator that one's self-esteem and self-worth are likely damaged, at a very low point, or worse, not even measurable. The search for a challenge is a search for the right medicine to soothe the pain and, in the process, restore one's damaged self-worth. The best prescription to stay away from this attraction is to stop looking for a challenge and start *being* one.

CHAPTER 10

"I Can Fix Him" Case Studies

Why would a woman want to have a relationship with a man she has to fix, especially when he's a bad boy? Why not aspire to find a man who is drama-free, stress-free, and who requires little to no maintenance? It's like going to a store and purchasing an item that you have to put together while the one right next to it is already assembled and ready for use—all that's left to do is to enjoy it. An even more intriguing question is what happens if, or should I say *when*, "fixing him" doesn't work? Few would disagree that these are rational and logical questions to what clearly has all the signs of behavior that must be added to the problematic and risky list. Yet we know this trend exists with far too many women, often leaving most of them psychologically and emotionally damaged. The good news is that as we turn up the volume of the "I can fix him" case studies, the genesis of this risky behavior begins to surface. And thanks to the high-definition view, these most compelling stories provide the basis for the antidote to "I can fix him."

On the surface, one could reasonably argue that understanding a woman's "fix him" attraction to bad boys requires no more than commonsense reasoning—it's a slam dunk, a no-brainer. After all, it is generally believed that women are nurturers by nature and as a result are inclined to behave in this manner. Case closed! No need to look any further! We can move on to the next case study! Not so fast! Not so fast because this common view changes drastically as the "I can fix him" experiences unfold. In fact, as each case study is told, it becomes increasingly clear that the bottom line is "I can fix him" is not really about "I can fix him," and the suspected link to nurturing is not really about nurturing.

"Conventional thinkers need not apply" is the initial message that emerges from just an overview of the case studies. To gain the most beneficial perspective, and thus learn from this fascinating attraction, it's going to take a little thinking outside the box. Few, if any, of the dynamics of why women want to fix their bad boy fit easily into a commonsense way of thinking. The mindset behind this behavior comes from several nonrelated directions, often originating from some unexpected or unforeseen sources. Keeping this in mind will make the ultimate goal of translating these enlightening personal experiences into life-changing solutions. While this may sound like the end game for discerning and then replacing such risky conduct, this is really where everything begins.

Not many would pick Dad as their first choice, and maybe even their second choice for that matter, as a primary reason behind the "I can fix him" mindset. For others, Dad being at the root of this mentality would most likely not even be on their radar. But the fact of the matter is that this is exactly the case. And dads make much more than just cameo appearances in these narratives. In effect, dads play a significant role in *all* of the case studies of the "I can fix him" phenomenon.

Before I could finish asking my initial question of why she was attracted to her bad boy to "fix him," Kelli immediately, and without the slightest hesitation, began with her dad—an interesting first reaction considering the question was asked about her bad boy. This bears repeating! I asked her about her bad boy and she told me about her dad.

Let's start with my dad. In terms of how he made me feel and how I had to prove myself to be worthy of his love, I was just reenacting with this guy [bad boy] . . . because, just like my dad was unavailable, so was this guy; just like my dad would call me names, so would this guy; just like my dad got a little physical, so would this guy.

You don't have to be a trained psychologist to see the parallels here. Kelli's relationship with her dad was plainly not a good one. It surely wouldn't qualify for the father-daughter hall of fame. And because the relationship with her dad never improved or was repaired, it was incomplete. A relationship that is incomplete needs closure before the affected person or persons can move forward with that part of their life. This is one of the main reasons so many people are emotionally and even physically stuck when it comes to functioning successfully in their personal relationships. Generally, where there is no closure, there is no peace. It's a lot like this thing that's just dangling out there flowing to and fro, around and around with no clear direction. Therefore, to fix this ever-looming problem, at least to the degree that some level of closure is realized, Kelli needed to engage in a relationship where there were enough similarities to create a sense of closure, albeit a false one. And the manner in which she chooses to find her peace of mind reflects the degree to which dads can impact their daughters' risky behavior in choosing their men.

Since Kelli had unresolved problems with her dad not being "available," she had to find a guy who was not "available" to "fix" this situation. Since Kelli's dad would call her names, she would only settle for a guy who would also do that to remove the emotional and psychological damage caused by this infraction. And finally, since her dad got "a little physical" with her, she sought out a guy who would do likewise, yet again, to remove the pain and suffering this caused her. She left no doubt that she was only acting this out because in her own description, she referred to her bad boy relationship as a "reenactment."

A rather tall Caucasian woman, perhaps an inch or two shy of six feet, Kelli, in her early thirties, had a take-charge personality. She was a student nearing completion of graduate school, assertive and presented as being somewhat upbeat. But this was so contrary to what her story depicted—a woman trapped and consumed in a state of helplessness. Nonetheless, the scars were real, and the pain was obvious as she constantly navigated through a web of emotions that pointed to her struggles with issues of self-worth and self-confidence in her relationship. After a lengthy interview, the last thing that Kelli said was "I need my dad to tell me he's sorry." She started the interview talking about her dad and ended her story talking about her dad. It seemed that her dad was the bookends to her life. The fact that she needed him to apologize to her indicates just how deep the issue of her dad was embedded into her psyche. Since Kelli wasn't able to fix her issues with her dad, she tried to accomplish this by attempting to fix them through her bad boy.

Christie's bad boy experience revealed what I refer to as a double dad issue. According to her account, her bad boy's dad was a lot like her own dad:

> John's dad was a lot like mine. He got divorced when he was young. I feel so sorry for him. His mother abandoned him and moved to another state with another man. I feel like if I fix John, then he's going to be perfect for me.

At the very least, not unlike Kelli, Christie recognized her own dilemma in her bad boy's situation. Her initial response, "John's dad was a lot like mine," all but confirms this. Once again, we see a situation where at the very outset, the response about a young woman's "I can fix him" relationship begins with her dad even though the initial question was about her bad boy. The only difference in

Christie's case is that she uses the bad relationship between her boyfriend and *his* dad to unload what was really at the core of her own deeply troubling issue—*her* dad. Different scenario, same outcome. At any rate, it's the development of the pattern that's important because it enhances our understanding of how this phenomenon works in the mindset of women. And the sharper the understanding, the more women will be able to write their own get-out-of-jail ticket. Let's take a look. Christie says that she "feels so sorry for him [John]." Since her bad boy's story is a lot like her own, then it seems rather obvious that Christie's feeling sorry for him is also her feeling sorry for herself. Equally enlightening is that Christie believes that if she can fix John, then "he's going to be perfect for me." The recount of her bad boy experience appears to be an unconscious reflection of her inner thoughts about herself—it was like a mirror reflecting back; therefore, "he's going to be perfect for me" is more like "I'm going to be perfect for me." If she could fix John, she would in essence be fixing herself. Fix herself from what, you may ask? Well, we can begin with self-doubt, self-pity, and bottom-shelf self-esteem.

Another intriguing aspect of Christie's story was that her bad boy was married to another woman at the same time she was having an affair with him. Looks like he was "bad boying" them both! Interestingly, this wasn't disclosed until near the end of the interview, which was most likely because this was a very uncomfortable subject for her to discuss. This became very noticeable as Christie, a soft-spoken twenty-two-year-old single white mom, continued to disclose her feelings on this subject. Her anger clearly escalated as she struggled through sharing the complications and difficulties of being the other woman. And just when I thought the anger had reached its peak, it intensified even more when she shared that she had a child by her bad boy. And if that wasn't enough, her anger reached a crescendo when she revealed that her bad boy denied it was his child and wanted no part of the infant.

Nita, a Native American, was a woman of deep reflection and spirituality. She had no problem and actually relished looking deep within herself to exam her own behavior. And much to her credit, she had no problem being accountable for those things that she discerned amounted to irresponsible behavior on her part. Nita's story had one of those "been there, done that" type of affects, especially within the context of all of the "I can fix him" case studies collectively:

> I felt that deep down he was a good person. He was abused as a child. He told me about how his dad would kick him out the house and beat him in the head and almost killed him. He had anger issues. I wanted to help him with that. I felt I could make him a better person than he was in terms of like he was very irresponsible. I felt that his cheating somehow would get better.

The mindset behind Nita's "I can fix him" behavior is also directed at Dad. But unlike Kelli and Christie, she mainly talks about her bad boy's dad for the most part. This was different. The pattern was about to be broken. At least this is what I thought throughout most of the interview. But then, just when it seemed the similarities in stories were about to face its first major distinction, just when it seemed that the patterns were not as ironclad as I thought, it turned out I was wrong. The only difference in Nita's story was that she didn't mention her dad until near end of the interview. No dad up front such as in Kelli's and Christie's case, but in Nita's case, he sure wasn't too far behind. Nita's dad was basically in and out of her life as she was growing up. The outs were more than the ins. But just like Kelli and Christie, the sense of abandonment and trust issues were not far behind either. And these very same emotions were displayed in Nita's demeanor as she discussed these extremely sensitive issues.

Being a very spiritual person, one who consistently looks inside herself for answers, it was clear that Nita took abandonment personally. Nita was in her midthirties but projected a maturity way beyond her years. She responded to her inner pain with the seriousness that would be associated with her level of maturity. Of course, this would once again bring on the need for closure because abandonment, which is frequently accompanied by trust issues, is often linked to distressing psychological issues. Nita's attempt to obtain closure was once again similar to those of Kelli and Christie—she would use her bad boy as an avenue through which she could find some level of relief and comfort. Specifically, Nita tried to remove her discomfort and find closure by forgiving her bad boy for cheating, saying, "I felt that somehow his cheating would get better." Based on the evidence provided from previous case studies, it seems reasonable to conclude that Nita's forgiving her bad boy for cheating was basically an unconscious, if not a conscious, way of forgiving her dad for abandonment—for not being there just like her bad boy wasn't there when she needed him. And be not deceived, from a psychological perspective, when the dad is not present in a woman's life, it is not unreasonable for her to view this as cheating and therefore abandonment. To be clear, we are not talking about cheating in a sexual sense but rather in a leaving or desertion context. In other words, if a dad is not present in his daughter's life, she feels that he is most likely with another woman, and therefore, in that framework of thinking, he is cheating on his daughter—he left her for another woman.

In the first fifteen to twenty minutes of the interview with Alexis, I thought that she and Nita must have talked and shared their stories. Of course, I knew that wasn't possible because there was no way they could know each other, but the progression with which they chose to present their personal experience with their bad boy was amazingly similar. Like Nita, Alexis didn't mention her dad until we were well into the interview, and the way she introduced him into her story had "defense mechanism" written all over it. But once she brought him into the discussion, the outward signs of the deep pain and emotions that I had become accustomed to seeing were not far behind:

My father was always there so it wasn't nothing dealing with my father or my parents. I've always seen them doing special things with each other. It was a fun household, we always had fun.

At this point I asked, "So there were no dad issues with you?" And Alexis did what amounted to a total about-face and said:

> You know what, it [relationship with Dad] might have played a part, 'cause when I was in middle school, my father actually divorced from my mother. Like what happened was, like, one day I woke up and he gave me a kiss like he usually do. I had to cheerlead at a game that evening and my grandfather picked me up and I remember saying, "This is awkward." When I got home my father had taken all his stuff and after that he was gone.

Two very different stories told within minutes of each other by the same person were most intriguing but not unusual for people suffering from abandonment and trust issues. What I just witnessed was a person who was in such deep and desperate denial that it was necessary to first paint a picture of what they wanted or needed to be in their reality. However, as she became more comfortable, she apparently decided to just come clean. It is not unreasonable that the pain was so difficult to deal with that she actually suppressed the fact that her dad left her—or at least in her mind, he left her. But her recalling something as significant as this, fifteen to twenty minutes after portraying a happy family, suggests that her issues were on a level that most psychologists would consider very serious.

To verify this point, Alexis was asked, "Did you forgive your dad for leaving you?" She nods her head that she hasn't forgiven him. I then asked if she would mind actually saying it instead of just moving her head. She complied with my request, saying, "No, I have not forgiven him." She then began to cry but after a few moments continued, saying:

Only because like, when he left he just left. And he left again after that. With my current boyfriend, when we have our arguments, I catch myself telling him, "You know, I don't have that male support. And I need you to kind of help with my emotions because my father never did that." Like I didn't have that father-daughter bond, like I really, really wanted.

Notice that at this point, Alexis has totally opened up and began dealing with what was really troubling her, saying, "I didn't have that father bond like I really, really wanted." It comes as no surprise that what Alexis was conveniently avoiding was once again abandonment and trust issues. This pattern has become so commonplace that now we could reasonably predict the circumstances under which a woman is likely to struggle with abandonment and trust issues when they are operating under the "I can fix him" attraction.

Alexis, an African American woman who was in her late twenties, seemed to have her work life and her school life under control and was moving in a positive direction. But in the area of interpersonal relationships, Alexis's life was a mess. It was far from positive because the psychological fallout of the "I can fix him" mentality was really taking its toll on her self-worth.

Unlike most of the "I can fix him" stories, Rebeca never once mentioned her dad. And even several attempts to bring up the subject were met with dead silence. The facial expressions were such that it sent the message any attentive researcher would understand: *do not go there*. Nonetheless, Rebeca was a twenty-two-year-old single Hispanic woman. She wanted to fix her bad boy so bad that for the better part of two years, she was literally taking care of him—that is, supporting him. This is not that unusual for many "I can fix him" women.

He would get jobs and either quit them or get fired. But I would never know the complete story of what happened.

It irritated me because I feel like I shouldn't be the only one working—this is supposed to be a 50/50 relationship. I shouldn't be the only one purchasing everything for us.

When asked how long did she do this, and whether she was still doing it, she replied, "Not at much but yes." It was also revealed in the interview that Rebeca's bad boy practically lived with her and her mom:

> He practically lives with me, lives with us. I made an agreement with him that he can come over on the weekends but on weekdays you have to stay home. I'm in school, I'm working full time. I don't have time to come home and you're not working and I still have to come home and do the laundry or my bed not be fixed and you haven't done anything all day. I wish my mom would be a little more strict on me about this but she likes him.

Notice that Rebeca realized her behavior was questionable, but for some reason she cannot bring herself to take any corrective action. She is actually looking for her mom to help her get out of this bad relationship. Rebeca was born in the United States, but her family is originally from the Dominican Republic. She was one of the more difficult interviews. Even though she volunteered, she seemed to struggle as she told her story.

I asked Rebeca, "Why did you put up with this, and did you think you could turn him around?" To this she replied:

> I guess I was trying to give him chances. I'm that kind of person who doesn't want to hurt feelings or break hearts, but it's nobody's fault but mine because I allow it. As far as did I think I could turn him around, well, um, I guess you could say that, yes. I just wanted to help him. Help him become a better person even if we weren't

together I wanted to help him. . . . I don't feel I'm doing
this for me but I do get self-gratification. It just feels good
to have helped somebody.

It appears that Rebeca's nurturing instinct had blinded her to
the point where she doesn't realize two important things about
her thinking and behavior. First, it is extremely difficult, if not
impossible, to change someone who is clearly not trying to help
themselves. And secondly, her comment that "I don't feel I'm doing
this for me, but I do get self-gratification" is plainly an example of
twisted and irrational thinking. This is what I call comfort-zone
processing. She does something that is gratifying but then says "I'm
not doing it for me." This reasonably raises the following question:
would she do it if she didn't get this self-gratification? If we consider
the pleasure, reality, and executive principles of Sigmund Freud's
theory of personality, the answer would most likely be NO!

Rachel started her recount with "I really didn't have a relationship
with my mom and still don't." No need to ask what was first and
foremost on her mind. When she continued, she shared the following:

I started noticing that he didn't have a relationship
with his family either. And I'm a caring person so I would,
you know, what's wrong, trying to play like a motherly
role–type thing. He began selling drugs at an early age.
His family life was broken. I mean he had no money, no
finances. I was like, oh, this has to be his only way, so I
have to help him. So that's what I did, I helped him sell
these drugs.

Rachel was in her midtwenties and from a mixed background.
She was very emotional when she shared her bad boy experiences. In
fact, she cried several times during the interview. She seemed to share
some of the same qualities that Rebeca displayed because it appeared
that her nurturing instinct got in the way of rational thinking and

therefore convinced her to perform the extremely risky behavior of helping her bad boy sell drugs. But to her credit, deep inside, Rachel knew that her conduct was problematic at the least:

> Even after that happened though [started to help him sell drugs] I did not think I was in the wrong. I felt like I was helping him . . . but all the while I was hurting myself.

When asked why she felt she had to help him, she replied, "Because I grew up with a broken family. He grew up with a broken family too, but unfortunately for him, he didn't have other family members to turn to." If there ever were solid evidence that the fixer was often the one needing fixing, here it was. What Rachel was essentially saying was he didn't have a relationship with his dad and mom, and she didn't have a relationship with her mom. "I came from a broken home, and he came from a broken home. If I can help him fix his broken home, I will, in essence, at least in my mind, be fixing my broken home."

We're not done yet with dads. Bridget, a youthful and humorous white woman in her early twenties, claimed she didn't know that the first male friend she had was a bad boy. But once again, as her story unfolded, the similarities continued to illustrate the patterns associated with this attraction as with the others.

> His dad had just left his mom and he had really low self-esteem. So he got me to do drugs with him. He was insecure and I thought I could fix that. He was a momma's boy. I thought I could make him happy and kind of fill the void that his dad left him in his life.

According to Bridget, her dad did not abandon her, nor did he abuse her, but what he did do could very well be considered a psychological kind of abandonment or abuse—he very rarely interacted with his daughter on any level. This could be an even more distressful situation because Bridget's dad was sitting right in the house, right in her presence, but hardly ever communicated with his daughter. It was plain to see that this had a very negative impact on her as she frequently commented on this noninteraction throughout the interview. So, by Bridget's own account, it appears that her dad left a huge void in her life by rarely communicating with her. Her response to this was to "kind of fill the void that his [her bad boy's] dad left him in his life." Once more, we see the pattern of how dads, even bad boy dads, take center court in influencing the risky social behavior of their children, especially their daughters. And not only does dad's influence play a major role in causing this conduct, but also, unfortunately, this behavior is often repeated. Just look at Bridget's second bad boy experience:

> His mom had passed away a year before I met him, and I felt I needed to fix him and take care of him. All the guys I've dealt with kind of had family issues growing up.

Bridget's addiction to thug love was so bad that she shared her experiences with a third bad boy:

> His mother was mentally challenged. This apparently took its toll because his dad left his mom and is now living with another woman. I feel like George kind of felt like his [sic] was left in the dust . . . by his dad.

Since Bridget had three bad boys with practically identical situations, I asked this question: "All three of your guys have been left by their parents. Do you see a pattern here? Tell me what you see." Bridget responded, "Like I don't like to be alone, and they don't like to be alone. I'm not attracted to guys who don't need me in that way because then I would feel unneeded." While Bridget's candor and honesty about her own behavior was refreshing, it is the "need me in that way" that is quite revealing. Bridget's need to be needed is so powerful that it totally dictates the type of person she will have a relationship with. Unfortunately, being such a slave to the need to be needed means that her criteria for a man is so narrow and limited that unless she changes her mindset, she will spend most of her life dealing with, and trying to fix, troubled men.

And just in case you thought that thug love was somehow restricted to heterosexual couples, think again. Erin was in a very intense lesbian relationship. She was an African American woman in her late twenties. Erin was an educated woman and was a hard worker as she was employed with more than one job. At the time of the interview, she was near completion of her master's degree. She was pushy with respect to having her story told. Keeping it real, she all but insisted that I hear her experiences and share them so that others can learn from her mistakes. The pain was easily recognizable. Like Lindsey, Erin could have been a multiple-attraction—"a challenge" and an "I can fix him"—candidate. However, it turned out that her challenge was in fact her desire to "fix" her partner:

> At that point in my life I was venerable and I just wanted to be with someone. And I was attracted to her, however, I realized that being in a relationship with her was a challenge for me. The challenge was this is someone who I would do things for that I would never do for a man.

Notice that at first Erin felt it was a challenge because she was struggling with her apparent desire to do things for her partner that she would never do with a man. These feelings were kind of new to her. But as the interview continued, it became clear that the challenge was much more than that when she described her feelings about her partner:

> She grew up feeling ugly. She didn't feel like she was pretty. I knew she was a horrible mother but I would tell her things to make her feel better.

Erin was trying to make her partner feel better by telling her untruths. This was her way of trying to fix her. The scene may be slightly different, but the mindset is the same as that of heterosexual couples. And this included abuse and cheating as well because Erin was one of the interviewees that I ended up counseling because the physical and psychological abuse between her and her partner became so severe that she ended up having to take out a court order on her.

A departure from the dad factor was not in the cards for the only LGBT couple in the research. Again, regardless of the makeup of the relationship, the script would not change, which once again confirms the universality of this phenomenon. Based on Erin's reflections of their relationship, her partner's dad was barely in her life. He had been in jail during most of her early childhood. Here is how she put it:

> Her father didn't, like, play any role in her life. He didn't come to her school. He didn't pick her up or drop her off. He was a hustler. During her early years he was in jail.

When asked about her own dad, Erin remarked:

> My father, he was around, but he wasn't around . . . you know what I mean? Fifty percent of the time he was there, and fifty percent of the time he wasn't there. He lived a double life.

Just like the majority of the other case studies, dads not playing an active role in their daughters' lives is a very sensitive subject. Erin would raise her voice every time the subject of her dad came up in the interview. Her dad issues and her partner's dad issues raised the anger level within each of them to the point that it tipped over into their daily interaction, causing friction, distrust, and, finally, mistreatment.

While dads have taken up most of the conversation thus far, there are other similarities and differences with the "I can fix him" experiences that offer additional insight into this phenomenon. For example, on the topic of drugs or jail, all the women—that's correct: *all* the women—tell stories of drugs being involved in their relationships on some level. Just a few will suffice. Kelli's bad boy had been to jail on several occasions for possession and selling drugs. Christie's bad boy also spent a little time in jail. Bridget said, "I soon found out that he was really bad into drugs because he had a lot of issues growing up like his parents divorced. So he got me to do drugs with him. I got really bad into drugs, and my parents sent me away to rehab." When I asked Bridget why she got so deep into drugs, she said, "I think it's a mix of my low self-esteem, my curiosity, and my lack of education in terms of drugs issues."

On the subject of sex and pregnancy, three of the five volunteers had children or got pregnant by their "I can fix him" bad boys. Bridget said that her bad boy denied the baby she was pregnant with, which was the reason she left him. She later had a miscarriage. Kelli acknowledged that the sex was very good and that *this most likely played a big role in how she approached her bad boy relationship.* To this end, she said:

> There have been times where like you know what, I don't need him as my man, I just want to you know. It's like part of me, it's kinda like Kelli come on, you know better than that, but the other half of me is like you know what, screw it, I'm a woman, and I have needs, and I know where to get it, and it's good, and if I can just, like, turn the volume down on the emotional side of this, I'll be alright.

Christie's described her sex life as follows: "All we did was have sex every day, sometimes several times a day." She would later go on to say:

Attention! I've got to have attention! I feel like if I have sex with them, then they want me and if they want me, then it's like a power that I guess I feel, like, in my mind that they want me. If I have something they want, if they want me, then that makes me feel good, that makes me feel wanted, that makes me feel important, that makes me feel loved, that makes me feel secure.

On the topic of sex with Bridget, she revealed, "Even after we broke up, we still had sex for a while." Nita was the only one who said that the sex wasn't that good.

When the topic of cheating came up, all but one of the women reported being cheated on. In Nita's case, the cheating started right after she got married. "I had some inward feelings to stay away but I wouldn't listen. . . . He slept with my roommate. I found notes from other women." And we can't overlook Nita's story when she said, "I felt that his cheating somehow would get better." Kelli described her experience with being cheated on, saying, "My boyfriend cheated on me with a woman who was much younger than him." Kelli recalls actually meeting the other woman whom she refers to as a girl and has even talked with her. While Christie reported that her bad boy cheated on her, she quickly added that she cheated on him as well. There is little doubt that this was clearly a defensive measure used by Christie to get back at him—all in an effort to try to ease the pain that being cheated on made her feel.

When the discussion turned to abuse, we know that Kelli's bad boy would abuse her at times: "Just like my dad got a little physical, so would this guy." Bridget's first bad boy physically abused her:

One time he saw a text message from another male friend and would just lose it and hit me. He would never beat me, he would just hit me. I don't think he ever hit me in the face.

Christie's bad boy was physically abusive, especially when he was drinking. On one instance, the physical abuse caused Christie to black out. His violence eventually landed him in jail. Nita's spin on abuse was as follows: "And as soon as he got married to me, it was more like a . . . mental abuse, everything changed. At that point, it was like he didn't care."

Even the differences—those things that were unique to each story—had touches of similarities, especially with regard to the common mindset that what women really wanted and needed was to fix themselves. Kelli was the only one to mention having a "phoenix complex." In describing what she meant by this, she said, "This basically means creating a chaotic situation in order to have something to fix up. This way I can say, 'Look at me, I did it, I'm okay, I made it through all of that, and I am still okay.'" She also made this eye-opening comment: "If I go to the dark side and I bring them to the light, then I was enough." It is clear from these two comments whom Kelli is really trying to fix. And we can't leave out Christie, the only one who was emphatic and extremely direct about attention. "Attention! I've got to have attention! I feel like if I have sex with them, then they want me, and if they want me, then it's like a power that I guess I feel, like in my mind that they want me." The power that Christie was referring to cannot be experienced without being fixed. It's clearly a "me" thing. Also, Christie's need for attention is secured through having sex with her partner, and with the use of "they," it appears that she had experienced this with more than one partner.

What needs to be fixed is not easily visible from just a surface view. From the outset, the stories point outward towards the bad boy while beneath the surface, these same stories reflect back to that more inward need. All the evidence seems to point to the fact that the "fix him" attraction is a type of mirror attraction. And since the women who shared their stories didn't like what they saw in the mirror, it became a mirror-avoidance issue. This may explain why, with the exception of Kelli and Christie, most of these young ladies did not discuss their dads until later, sometimes much later in their bad boy recounts. Dealing with emotionally painful issues, especially interpersonal relationship issues, is not something most welcome with open arms. It's not unusual for people to avoid facing difficult and painful personal problems. When you factor in the high degree of sensitivity that dad issues bring to the mix, avoidance could actually be an attractive alternative—although it will have a kick-the-bucket-down-the-street affect. When this occurs, it is often manifested in what is known in psychology as a projection—a Freudian defense mechanism which means that instead of tackling an issue head-on, people often project their pain and fears on others to soften the blow. Bridget's comment is a good illustration of projection: "Like I don't like to be alone, and they don't like to be alone." She starts out trying to deal with her pain by acknowledging it, but because this burden is so heavy, she immediately projects her feelings of loneliness in her boyfriend's direction by saying he doesn't like to be alone also. At this point, the unwanted feelings are pushed to the unconsciousness so the individual will not have to deal with it. Burying these feelings in the unconsciousness is one reason why it's hard for the individual to see themselves in such situations. And to a large degree, this is why the rampant abuse and cheating we have seen so often continue for so long.

Another important psychological factor relative to the "I can fix him" phenomenon is known as "repetitive relationship patterns of behavior," which explains why these women revisit their risky behavior time and time again. Sometimes referred to as a deceptive or menacing phenomenon, Sigmund Freud described it as "repetition compulsion." To be clear, this is a neurotic-type disorder which again falls under Freud's well-known psychosocial theory of defense mechanisms. And it is exhibited by the harmed or affected person trying to rewrite history, mainly from troubled relationships in families. This happens more so with parents than siblings, and especially the opposite-sex parent, which is exactly what we have seen in every "I can fix him" case study.

Dads! Dads! Dads! If case studies can lead to the whodunit in solving the mysteries of thug love, dads are the leading suspects—not just suspects, but the leading suspects. This doesn't mean that dads are the only ones responsible for the risky behavior of their daughters; however, all the evidence does point to him being a major factor. If dads would only realize the impact, especially emotionally, that they have on their children, particularly their daughters, one would think they would try to clean up their act. It almost seems unreal that what is behind the scene in practically each case study is a bad relationship between a father and a daughter. What's even more frightening is how this works with respect to mindset; that is to say that women tend to try to work out their dad problems with their bad boys.

Whether it was Kelli or Christie, Nita, Alexis, Bridget, Rebeca, Rachel, or Erin, the lived experiences of women caught in the "I can fix him" sweepstakes contains remarkable and revealing stories that transcends conventional thinking. Make no mistake, nurturing is a subtle factor in the "I can fix him" mentality. But when you look at the bottom line with respect to discerning this mindset, Kelli said it best when asked, "Do you love him? Do you love him in spite of everything he's done?" "Yeap! Yeap! I love this man because he is; he is a representation of my fantasy." And, of course, we know now that this fantasy also comes with instructions for healing women in thug love: take the "him" out of "I want to fix him," and replace it with "me": "I want to fix me."

From surveys to case studies and from discussions with small groups to large groups, we have examined many of the problems and issues associated in dealing with bad boys. Now we must turn our attention to getting those Help Wanted signs down. Thus, the remaining chapters will be devoted to dealing directly with solutions. And considering the wealth of information we have been able to collect, finding solutions will be not be that difficult as they will practically find us. But even with many of the answers virtually jumping out at us, the next step of actually changing the risky behavior of thug love will not be an easy task. In fact, changing behavior on any level is almost always a daunting endeavor and is therefore most effective when using the psychological perspective.

CHAPTER 11

The Psychology Of
Dealing With Bad Boys

Tips, Tactics, and Theories

The mindset is a terrible thing to ignore. As social interaction takes place in our lives day in and day out, the mindset is the hub of all these experiences. It guides and directs our behavior. It elevates or lowers our self-esteem. It can require more or settle for less. It can shape or shatter our dreams and aspirations. And it determines who is successful and who is not. Unfortunately, the mindset can also be manipulated. In thug love, this is often the case as bad boys are aware of the woman's vulnerabilities and are skillful enough to use their swag, sex appeal, and just plain old smooth talk to influence the woman's thinking on many levels. Thus, the bad boy is able to destroy their self-esteem, distort their reality, play on their emotional insecurities and weaknesses, and even convince them to settle for less. All of these lower the bar to the point where in the women's mindset the bad boy is not required or even held responsible for helping to cultivate, nurture, or advance the relationship. This explains, at least in part, why the majority of women who try to get out of thug love often fail, or even worse, return for more rounds of irresponsible behavior. If this is not being brainwashed, it's surely close. But even in the face of mostly negative outcomes in bad boy relationships, the reality is if you can change the mindset, which continues to be our goal, you can change the behavior. The negative can be turned into a positive. And at the center of this dynamic is the psychology of dealing with bad boys because where there is behavior, there is psychology.

Why psychology? First, psychology is multidimensional. The goal of psychology is to describe, explain, predict, control, and change behavior. In light of the multidimensional nature of thug love, the psychological perspective pulls the covers off the many facets of the behavior associated with this phenomenon. In doing so, the power of the psychological perspective arms women with the tools for developing a well-rounded, system-rooted, and reliable course of action, one that will ultimately remove the Help Wanted signs. And with this knowledge and insight, women will be able to use these tools to either get away from the grasp or entirely evade the lure of the bad boy. But change within itself is not enough. It must be a change that can be sustained over time because with the debilitating effects of thug love, one thing we cannot afford is repeat victims. This only further damages the mindset, rendering it even more difficult to transform or change the desired behavior. Psychology's holistic approach will not only map out the prescription of *what* to do to escape or avoid this lifestyle but also *how* and *why* it should be done as well. While tips are a good way to begin this process, understanding the psychology of dealing with bad boys means not only providing help with *tips* but also with *tactics* and *theories* as well.

Second, psychology is research- and reality centered—opinions matter, but facts reign. The psychological perspective focuses more on facts than opinions unless those views are supported by—you guessed it—facts! One of the reasons why thug love is so hard to overcome is because many women are bombarded with the opinions of friends and relatives. This is not to discount the value of the support of family and friends as they can be helpful to a point when going through struggles and handling difficult personal situations. But considering the complex nature of the emotions and attitudes involved in dealing with bad boys, women need facts—something they can hold on to and believe will make a difference as they navigate through the challenging task of changing their risky behavior. The case studies have provided us with a rich and well-rounded look at some of the realities of thug love. When this kind of rich information is available, it acts as a motivator because with such knowledge the woman can be confident that whatever corrective measures she employs, she'll be on the right track. As more and more women begin to understand the value of viewing their behavior through the psychological perspective, they will find that reliable and valid information allows them to construct a behavioral change program that will produce not just results but permanent results as well.

Finally, psychology is theory- and principle based. From what we have learned thus far, the behavior of both the woman and the bad boy often points to some of the major theories and principles of psychology. This is significant because these theories are rooted and grounded in sound and proven principles, which widens the scope of potential help—and it is no secret that women in thug love need all the help they can get. Some of the behaviors that stand out include the psychology of learned helplessness; assimilation and accommodation; positive and negative reinforcement; the need to belong as put forth in Maslow's hierarchy of needs; top-down, bottom-up processing; and Sigmund Freud's theory of the id, ego, and superego. A good example of how theories and principles can help is that thug love would largely be studied under the subfield of social psychology, which observes how we interact with each other in social settings. However, at the same time, thug love could be investigated within the confines of another field of psychology—counseling psychology—as the person acting out the risky behavior involved in these relationships will most likely have a need for some degree of counseling or therapy. There are a number of other subfields in psychology that could apply as well. They include but are not limited to clinical psychology, educational psychology, developmental psychology, and even biopsychology. We know from the *why* of psychology that with this powerful behavioral discipline we can describe, predict, control, and change behavior. It is equally important that we understand *how* psychology accomplishes this as well.

From most psychological perspectives, behavior is usually observed or monitored over a period of time—days, weeks, months, even years. This almost always produces patterns of human conduct and actions. Once patterns are established, predicting behavior becomes an easy task as patterns of human conduct are often repeated, leaving clear and identifiable relationships. And as behavior can be predicted in light of patterns, it can be controlled and thereby changed. In other words, if we know something is coming, like an unwanted behavior, this prior knowledge provides enough information to take corrective or avoidance measures. Imagine the many ways that the *how* of psychology can benefit women trapped in thug love.

To begin with, keeping it real, which psychological research does, has built-in safeguards that will not allow the truth to be distorted or misrepresented. The truth has commanding liberating power wherein the woman in thug love will eventually realize, as most of them do, that the only way out is to embrace the truth no matter how difficult it may be. As this becomes a reality, a key process in changing their behavior is activated—thinking. This cognitive function is vital because now the woman is thinking, and to change a person's behavior, they must first change their thinking. The level of discernment that is associated with truthful thinking and reasoning will almost certainly lead to a sense of responsibility. And this is major because the woman in thug love cannot begin the change process until she first accepts responsibility for the role that she played in getting into relationships where she is now trying to modify her behavior

We noted earlier that the theories and principles of psychology are key! From manufacturing to agriculture, from education to technology, there are principles that must be applied in these and other areas of production. There are certain basic steps that must be followed to make a quality automobile or to grow the best crops, lesson plans to teach our children, and the ones and zeroes which are the backbone of our computer technology. This is also true in psychology. The principles and theories in psychology provide a systematic process that helps us comprehend and sort out the behavior on a number of levels, from which the ultimate goal of changing behavior can be achieved. One example is Maslow's hierarchy of needs. Here, various stages of human needs are placed in a logical one-step-at-a-time framework which we all must experience before going on to the next level of meaningful life. And if these needs are not met—physical needs, security needs, and the need to belong—we are stuck at that respective stage and therefore unable to progress to the next level. If Maslow's "need to belong" level is not satisfied, the person will not be able to realize the next level which is a healthy self-esteem. We have seen how this affects women in thug love because so many of them behave in ways where it is obvious that they have little self-worth. Another example of how understanding some of the basic theories of behavior can be helpful in rooting out thug love is the principle of assimilation and accommodation. Simply put, assimilation is basically trying to "fit in" or adopting the practices of another culture, or in this case a lifestyle, regardless of what was previously believed, while accommodation involves actually changing or conforming one's behavior. We saw this from all three of the attractions where women assimilated or accommodated, or both for that matter, to have a relationship with their bad boys. Again, understanding these concepts from the psychological perspective provides the women in thug love with a down-to-earth framework from which to first understand and then modify her behavior. These and many more theories and principles have been used since psychology has been around and have been responsible for helping people from all walks of life make needed behavioral corrections in their lives involving anywhere from mild to severe psychological issues and disorders.

Finally, at one point in the study, I shared with a group of women that if they would only look at their behavior within the framework of some of the principles of psychology, they would discover the insight to pave the way to higher-quality relationships. And after a few more years of research, I became even more convinced that the road to changing risky behavior begins and ends with understanding the psychology of dealing with bad boys. Since the mindset can be manipulated to the bad boy's advantage, we must be ever mindful that the mindset can also be changed to the woman's gain. With this in view, and based on what has been revealed from this research and from the psychological perspective, I have developed seven tips, along with the tactics and theories that women in thug love can use in changing their risky behavior to more responsible behavior.

TIP NO. 1:
DISCONTINUE THE REWARDS PROGRAM

You can barely go shopping these days, in person or on the Internet, without a retailer trying to influence or shape your shopping behavior with some type of rewards program. In psychology, when a behavior is rewarded, it is commonly referred to as reinforcement. There are basically two types of reinforcement: positive and negative. Positive reinforcement occurs when you add a desirable or pleasant stimulus, and negative reinforcement occurs with the removal of an aversive or undesirable stimulus. Needless to say, positive reinforcement is the kind of reinforcement mainly, but not exclusively in play with, thug love. When the woman says yes to the thug love lifestyle, she is in essence rewarding the bad boy with what he desires, thus reinforcing his behavior. In her article "Why Do Men Fall for Bad Boys," Vinita Mehta writes:

> Research has revealed that more men than women possess the Dark Triad personality traits of narcissism, psychopathy, and Machiavellism. The hallmarks of narcissism include dominance, a sense of entitlement, and a grandiose self-view.

There is no doubt that the signs of narcissism—dominance, entitlement, and a grandiose view of self—is present in bad boys, but that is mainly because it is constantly reinforced by women. What this means is that the woman is actually supporting and even encouraging the bad boy not only to continue in his ways but also to continue having his way with his woman, or women. Unfortunately, this is a self-inflicted wound because while it finds the woman functioning as an enabler, nurturing the fertile soil upon which the bad boy's ego or narcissism consistently grows, it also causes her own self-worth to be deflated. It's a see-saw affect, albeit a one-way see-saw affect—the bad boy's ego is raised, while the woman's self-worth is lowered. And as these acts of reinforcement become routine in thug love relationships, it begins to function as a rewards program. Most women are usually unaware of the degree to which their own acts of reinforcement are promoting, sustaining, and, most importantly, advancing the bad boy phenomenon. Adding insult to injury, as the rewards program becomes a routine occurrence in the relationship, it ultimately becomes a matter of conditioning—another psychological principle which further promotes the rewards program.

To acquire relief from the self-inflicted wound of the rewards program, women must equip themselves with the tools to fight back. The obvious first step is to discontinue the rewards program. But before any level of success can be realized in this regard, a working understanding of how reinforcement and conditioning impacts thug love is necessary. A few examples are in order.

In the protection attraction, the rewards program strengthens and boosts the bad boy's ego because it reinforces the fact that he is needed as a protector while the woman pays the price for this protection by having to be under his control. In the "a challenge" attraction, the rewards program is one in which the bad boy is the recipient of the pleasurable stimulus of being sought after so the woman can ultimately feel like she is number one. Of course, she pays the price for this when she realizes there is no number one with a bad boy. And in the "I can fix him" attraction, the rewards program is fully operational when the bad boy enjoys the pleasurable stimulus of unwavering attention to correct what the woman feels needs fixing to make him a better man. The woman pays the price for this by never being given equal attention. Any way you look at it, this is a psychological hell. To avoid or escape this emotional purgatory, a psychological principle called extinction must be enacted.

The tactic of extinction occurs when the behavior is no longer reinforced. Theoretically, all the woman has to do is stop the rewards program as this change in her behavior will lead to a change in his behavior. Unfortunately, it's not quite that easy. When employing the tactic of extinction, especially where conditioning has occurred, there is the likelihood that this will be met with considerable resistance by the bad boy. After all, he has become used to being rewarded. It could even result in behavior ranging from ugly to possible violence depending on what has been allowed in the relationship over time. To avoid this, the woman who wants out bad enough will enact the extinction approach by implementing it gradually since in all likelihood the rewards program was applied in the same manner.

Another way to look at it is that it's a lot like supply and demand. As long as there is a demand for his services, the bad boy will be more than happy to supply the woman with what she needs or, in this case, what she thinks she needs. After all, his self-worth has been greatly inflated because he is well aware that his demand has gone up. When an automobile is popular and is in high demand, the manufacturer will make more cars to meet the demand. But if the manufacturer does not meet this demand, he will eventually go out of business. The bottom line is if you want the bad boy to go out of business, women will have to *discontinue the rewards program.*

TIP NO. 2:
RESPECT AND CHECK REALITY

Women under the grip of thug love have a difficult time recognizing and dealing with reality. This is usually manifested by the woman distorting, rationalizing, or outright denying the truth. In many cases, I have talked to women who clearly had a bad boy but denied being in a thug love relationship altogether. It was brought out earlier that in psychology, these actions are called defense mechanisms. Based on the psychoanalytic theory of Sigmund Freud, the unconscious mind uses psychological maneuvers to influence, deny, or distort reality. These maneuvers are considered defense mechanisms because they help the person maintain a social image that is generally considered acceptable in society. Speaking in the vernacular, it's like keeping face. Reversing this trend is paramount because it gives the women the best chance to change her risky behavior by respecting and checking reality. Understanding how diversions from reality begin and how they are sustained is most advantageous to reversing this trend.

In most instances, what goes on in thug love stays in thug love. Obviously this is a take on the old cliché "what goes on in Vegas stays in Vegas." While this concept may work well in Las Vegas, it certainly doesn't work well for the woman dealing with a bad boy. These often-deceitful relationships thrive on the bad boy keeping what goes on in his relationships only between him and his woman. Thus, the relationship functions mainly in a vacuum. Unfortunately, this provides an ideal environment from which to create a false reality. With the use of swag, charm, sometimes subtle or overt ultimatums, and even threats, the bad boy is able to separate the woman from those things that keep her connected to reality—her family and friends. This is similar to the concept of "divide and conquer." In any event, once this is accomplished, the mindset to accept a false reality is in place. We saw this with the protection attraction case studies when most of the women neglected or just plain left their families and friends to secure what they thought was protection from their bad boys. The isolation in these cases caused a diversion from the truth mainly because the cloudy residue left behind makes it difficult to recognize reality. We also saw this same thing with the challenge case studies, where the women would isolate themselves with their bad boy—either through deceitful persuasion or voluntarily—to experience excitement and adventure, but in reality, their thug love relationship turned out to be a rendezvous with drugs, sex, and abuse. Distorting, rationalizing, and denying their situations were all in play here as well. And finally, the "I can fix him" attraction, which supposedly was about fixing the bad boy, was in reality about the woman's need to get fixed.

Changing this risky behavior begins with developing a healthy respect for reality. The best tactic to realize this goal is reality checks. And with this, women can take back their reality, which will allow them to begin the process of modifying their behavior. On the other hand, the woman trying to avoid these relationships altogether will not allow a bad boy to make them lose sight of their real world because she is armed with the identifiers that will help her recognize the bad boy's intentions before he can do any harm. This is where the power of psychology of dealing with bad boys is so potent, and by the way, it's more powerful than the grip of thug love.

The psychological perspective provides the insight that lets the woman know exactly how and why her behavior poses a risk to her well-being and what steps can be taken to change this. First, through frequent reality checks, the woman will be able to see if any form of isolation exists in her relationship. If so, she will know to correct this immediately by staying in touch with family and friends, and doing so frequently. This should include making sure that she goes out on dates with other couples as frequently as possible. Interacting with others socially will help keep a person grounded in reality by comparing and contrasting what other couples are doing and how other couples are functioning. A note of caution here: be careful that your friends are not in the same boat as you; that is, they are not dealing with bad boys themselves.

Second, in keeping reality in check, the woman trying to get out of thug love must never deny or rationalize any form of abuse, be it verbal, psychological, or physical. Usually this is done by the woman to avoid losing the bad boy and is often manifested by her making the kind of excuses we heard in our case studies—he really didn't mean it or worse yet rationalizing being pushed around as not being physical abuse. The underlying cause of this behavior in large part is due to the woman not wanting to be viewed negatively by society. To prevent this, women should avoid allowing their reality to be shaped by others and thus prevent their behavior from being dictated by social pressures.

Finally, take the time to learn more about defense mechanisms. There are approximately fifteen of these so-called protective behaviors in psychology. For the most part, defense mechanisms are used by most of us to help us cope with daily stressors. This is more the reason why this psychological theory should be thoroughly comprehended. To the women in thug love or trying to avoid it altogether, the better this phenomenon is understood, the more respect women will have for the truth and the more women will be able to keep their reality in check.

TIP NO. 3:
LET THE BOTTOM BEFRIEND THE TOP

It has been said many times that a dog is man's best friend. This may very well be true where the man is involved, but to the women in thug love, her best friend is within. Unfortunately, most women rarely activate their friend within when it comes to dealing with bad boys. This is a huge mistake when someone is involved in an interpersonal relationship but one that can be corrected. Women are virtually always cast as being very emotional, which means that their behavior is largely governed through their senses—what they feel, see, hear, etc. From the psychological perspective, this principle or theory is known as bottom-up, top-down processing. The goal in this tip is for the senses to communicate and interact more with the mind. The research reveals that most of the behavior associated with thug love is sense driven. In other words, women tend to rely on how they feel and what they see as opposed to taking the time to mentally process what the actions of their bad boys really mean. The tactic to correct this is for the woman to let the bottom become friends with and depend more on the top—where critical thinking and problem solving occurs.

It is commonly accepted that most of our interaction with the world comes from the environment through our five senses. If we simply behave based on this information alone, we could easily misinterpret what we believe our senses are telling us and thus not receive the full benefit of our contact with the world. For example, if you go outside in the winter to sense how cold it is, this will certainly help you gauge how heavy a coat you will need. But if in conjunction with this, you look at the local weather report via television, radio, or other means, you may find out that the temperature will rise outside of the coat-wearing range later in the day. Now with this additional top-down information, you can better plan your day, and this will most likely change your behavior with respect to the way you will dress for the day. With the abundance of top-down information about bad boys available through this study, women now know enough to get out of thug love or avoid it altogether because they know that being cheated on is inevitable, that real protection is highly unlikely, that the fixer is the one who really needs fixing, and that from the psychological perspective their best friend is within.

TIP NO. 4:
QUALIFY YOUR NEEDS

What do you need? What do you really need? What do you really, really need? Notice the questions do not ask, "What do you want?" If the women trying to get out of thug love would address their needs instead of their wants, they could make their bad boy relationship a memory. We must revisit Maslow's hierarchy of needs once more for this tip because it is the psychological principle that is most effective. The need to belong is often overwhelming. The majority of all of us tend to allow our relationships, or the lack thereof, to define who we are and even how we feel about ourselves. All too often we let our standing among colleagues and peers be determined by whether we have a significant other in our lives or not. Don't get caught without a man, for society will eat you alive. When a woman's need to belong is not realized, that is to say she doesn't have a man, it is often interpreted as an issue or a shortcoming of the woman. It's not unusual to hear such comments, especially in woman circles, as "Why can't you keep a man?" or "Why are you having problems holding down a relationship?" Thug love is particularly susceptible to the need to belong not being realized by women primarily because these unpredictable relations are by definition "short-lived."

The need to belong reaches far into the human psyche. We have learned that it plays a pivotal role in self-esteem and self-worth, and we have seen that when one's self-esteem is damaged, it usually turns into irresponsible behavior. Note that it is not just belonging but rather the need to belong that we are dealing with here. According to Maslow's theory, the hierarchy of needs is presented in a pyramid of five levels of needs: physiological needs, security needs, love and belonging needs, esteem needs, and the need for self-actualization. If a certain level of need is not met, then the individual will not be able to proceed to the next level of the pyramid. The need to belong is the third tier of the pyramid, and if that need is not satisfied, the person will not be able to experience a rewarding level of self-esteem, which is the next level of the pyramid. This plays out true to form in most of our case studies. For example, women in the "a challenge" attraction experienced very low self-esteem. We know this because they regularly put up with their bad boy cheating on them as well as physically and psychologically abusing them. If they had a more positive view of themselves, this surely wouldn't have been allowed. Nonetheless, the desperation to fill the need for excitement and/or danger, or should I say a perceived need, frequently gets in the way of sound judgment and making good personal decisions. There is nothing more important than deciding whom to interact with on an intimate level and, even more importantly, whom *not* to interact with. When such an important decision is made in haste, especially in the dating world, danger will most certainly follow.

To avoid making such misguided judgments, women would best be served if they would qualify their needs. In doing so, the tactic is to construct a profile of the type of guy you need first, and then and only then can you add in a few wants. First, make sure you are not trying to get a man because your friends are putting pressure on you. Of course, if they are, they're not really your friends. Also, make sure your man-goals are realistic. Remember how our "a challenge" or protection attraction friends turned out. Second, make a needs chart, something like a grocery list. This will definitely keep you focused and on point. If on your list the man has to have a job and some education beyond high school—and he should—then you should not stray from these values under any circumstances. Remember, he can have all the swag in the world, but you can't pay bills with swag. Also, when a man can meet your high standards, this is usually a sign that he is forward thinking, that he is the kind of guy who is trying to make something out of himself—the kind of guy with whom you could possibly build a future. By the way, if you are going to have high standards, you might want to make sure that you can meet them as well. It's a lot easier to select or not select a guy when you have well-conceived and thought-out standards, and you have applied them to yourself as well. In other words, make sure you practice what you preach. This doesn't mean that women will not experience some weaknesses at times in holding true to some of their standards, but when some type of tangible objective is in place, it's a lot more difficult to breach one's values. After all, getting out or avoiding these dangerous relationships are ultimately matters of holding true to your standards and principles. Finally, observe Maslow's theory regularly. Write it down somewhere you know you will see it every day. This will keep you totally attentive to the mission of *qualifying your needs.*

TIP NO. 5:
SEEK TO BE OUT OF CONTROL

Most of the women in the protection case studies realized that they were getting more control than protection. If you recall, Candice, from one of the case studies on protection, said, "He really didn't protect me, but he controlled me for a while." Being controlled often leads to a loss of identity and a skewed view of reality. From the psychological perspective, being controlled is associated with learned helplessness, which is basically feeling that you can't control events and circumstances in your life. Sufferers often react passively to threats, failing to display "normal" signs of frustration or aggression. If they are bullied or taken advantage of, they are unlikely to fight back or complain. We discovered from some of our thug love case studies that women who desired bad boys for protection had to give up something, which, in most of cases, was family and friends. Separation from the family unit, whether voluntary or coerced, creates a strong sense of dependence on their protector. This quickly becomes a psychological state of conditioning. But what has been given must be taken back. The tactic here is to embrace and utilize the psychological principle of negative reinforcement to regain a sense of meaning and purpose in one's life. To do so requires removing the aversive stimulus, which in this case means reconnecting with family and friends. Of course, removing one's self from the bad boy altogether would be the preferred method, but realistically, this may not work for many women because thug love is a very powerful phenomenon, and pulling up stakes all at once could have negative consequences. Nonetheless, this is a good start for those who are already dealing with bad boys.

A word of caution: if by chance the woman has been living with her bad boy for a reasonable period of time—anywhere from three to six months or longer—she must be very careful when trying to get out of his control. The more control he has been accustomed to, the more resistant he will likely be to change. Depending upon the history and dynamics of the relationship, this could result in some stiff resistance, perhaps even some confrontation. If the control has been ironclad or exceptionally dominating, trying to regain a sense of independence all at once could be met with strong resistance. Therefore, similar to the tactics in tip no. 1, this approach must be implemented gradually, but to be clear, it must be implemented.

TIP NO. 6:
WATCH WHAT YOU EAT

They are glorified in music videos. They are hyped in magazines. And they are portrayed as seductive on billboards, on television, in movies, and, of course, through social media. All of this is designed to make the bad boy appealing to the woman, and it works! It's a matter of conditioning, and just like Ivan Pavlov's dog salivated even when the unconditioned stimulus was removed, women have been conditioned to "salivate" at the sight of the bad boy or any related icon. Classical conditioning is yet another psychological principle that if understood can be used to help women curb their appetite of bad boys.

I don't have to pull out the textbook on classical conditioning because the lived experiences of women in thug love have clearly illustrated how it works—how women have bought into the hype and seduction. For example, you may recall Terry from the "a challenge" case studies who said, "But, like, if I see something and, like, I kind of want it, like, I will go for it," or Georgia from the protection case studies who said, "I married someone who knew how to shoot and kill people." One of the first steps in becoming conditioned is seeing the unconditioned stimulus paired with the neutral stimulus. Even though they both had different reasons for dealing with bad boys, Terry and Georgia were conditioned—they bought into the hype. They both saw and consumed the product. In this case, it is the bad boy's persona of being a protector. There is an old saying that you are what you eat. Nothing could be more truthful. Frankly, women who know they can be easily led should avoid watching any form of media that glorifies bad boys. If these women cannot be disciplined in this regard, it will be most difficult to break the conditioning and thus break the hold that bad boys have on them. As mentioned earlier, in psychology, when you want to break the shackles of conditioning, the antidote is called extinction. It's like putting out a fire. It works when you make sure that the neutral stimulus has been removed. In this case, it is not only the image of the bad boy via all the usual media outlets but also what he is being paired with that must be avoided. It could be a car, certain clothes, an outfit, or even music. Whatever the case may be, you can be seduced. All of us have been conditioned to something. In my view, this is one of the most important principles in psychology. So much so that I have all of my undergraduate psychology students conduct a final exam project on classical conditioning in the media. Just think, conditioning is so effective that you don't have to see a McDonald's hamburger to want one. All you have to do is see the golden arches, and because of conditioning through television commercials and other advertising medium, you will immediately think of one of McDonald's products. Remember, if Pavlov's dog could be conditioned to salivate at the clicking of a metronome—with no food in front of him at all, might I add—then there is little doubt that this can happen to the best of us. Just look at it like this: if you don't put it in you, it won't have to come out of you. So *watch what you eat!*

TIP NO. 7:
INVEST IN A TIME SHARE FOR PERSONAL CARE

The flip side of the need to belong is not belonging. This is crucial because it basically means facing one of the most feared of all personal situations—being alone. Most people dread being alone, but there is an upside to being alone for the woman who is trying to get out of thug love. Being alone has therapeutic value. It is likely that one of the reasons women get into these nonproductive relationships is because she does not know herself, and of course, this is because she hasn't taken the time to do so. It is difficult to change this behavior while being around your friends and even your family because total transparency is needed to clearly see what makeovers need to be put into action. And you can't have total transparency unless you spend quality time alone. In psychology we call it introspection. This is where individuals take the time to examine their own conscious thoughts and feelings in an effort to better understand and even to question themselves. Some refer to it as soul-searching. Whatever the case, this is a powerful way to get control over one's behavior and thus a powerful way to get out in front of changing dangerous behavior. The tactic is to simply make a real investment in personal care, taking time away from everyone, at least every couple of months, for reflection and correction. This personal time will give you the opportunity to clean inside out which is where the real problems generally originate. To the woman who has a bad boy, this may not be easy to do, but it must be done if she is going to improve her situation. Go away! Go far away! Go to the mountains, to a beach resort! Go to an island if your funds permit, but go away! Go where there are as few people as possible. Put the cell phone away, and just be alone. This is when you can do your best soul-searching and reach that inner part of you where you won't be interrupted from cleaning house—strengthening weaknesses, arresting insecurities, and developing a healthy dose of confidence and self-reliance.

The tips and tactics set forth will undoubtedly provide a sound basis for executing the strategies and interventions that can be used by women to get out of bad relationships. But even after reviewing these sound help tips, it seemed like something was still missing.

The theories give added context and perspective which can be called on as reminders to help the woman stay out of bad relationships. But notwithstanding such serviceable concepts, it still seemed like more could be done. And even in light of all that has been uncovered through surveys, group conversations, and case studies, there continued to be a strong feeling that a deeper understanding of this phenomenon was still out there. The best description I can give is that it was a persistent inward desire to provide even more insight for women to not only be able to break loose from problematic behavior but to also move forward with the confidence of being able to have productive and meaningful relationships in the future.

After spending a considerable amount of time reflecting and meditating in this regard, several factors of the research resonated in my thinking. These factors provided the groundwork from which I developed three additional theories providing a deeper understanding of the genesis of the thug love mindset. With so much at stake in bad boy relationships, the development of any additional theories could only be of further help to our goals. One thing is for certain: it surely couldn't hurt because theories help to organize observations, stimulate inquiry, and show relationships. Thus, the three theories that I developed from this research are "the fear factor," "the seed factor," and "the choosee/chooser factor." The remaining chapters describe and examine these theories in the context of why women are attracted to bad boys.

CHAPTER 12

The Fear Factor

"The fear of being hurt" has been uttered more than any phrase since the research of thug love began. The frequency with which fear has been mentioned made it irresponsible if not impossible to ignore. The first few times the "fear of being hurt" was articulated, the connection between this fear and thug love didn't seem rational; as a result, it didn't show up on the radar screen. However, after hearing this phrase by women over and over again, it became apparent that this factor needed to be examined further. This being said, the first of our three theories deals with what I call the fear factor. When stated in classical theory terminology, fear contributes to the bad boy attraction and leads to risky and irresponsible behavior.

Fear is serious business on any level. Even in "mainstream" relationships there is empirical evidence which indicates that attachment issues, protection issues, and even self-worth issues can and are often linked to fear. For example, in a study of 125 ethnically diverse college women by Impett & Peplau (2002), they found that many students engaged in unwanted sex because they were afraid that their partners would lose interest in them. In other words, cut them back. It sounds like they borrowed a page from thug love. This is how it is stated in the study:

> As predicted, anxiously attached women were the most willing to consent to unwanted sex, and they often cited fears that their partner would lose interest in them as reasons for their compliance.

This easily confirms the power and impact that fear has on behavior in interpersonal relationships. And keep in mind that this is just with mainstream-type relationships.

Whether in large groups, small groups, or one-on-one interviews, one of the main goals in examining this theory became finding out exactly what do women mean when they say they are afraid of being hurt. Consequently, I have asked this question to women many times throughout this research. I have even called personal female friends to get some type of understanding on what it specifically meant by "being hurt." No one seemed to be able to paint the kind of picture I needed—one that would offer a description that could lead to a clear representation of the mental processes involved with this thinking. Women seem to understand it among themselves, but they just couldn't put it to words. They would nod their heads at each other during the discussions as though they were speaking a language that only women understood—some type of coded language exclusively between women. While persistently digging deeper, I was finally able to at least get an idea of what happens when the woman has actually been hurt. The most definitive responses over time included such things as "it's like this pain in your stomach" or "a lot of times you can't sleep at night" or "I know I can't stay focused and have a hard time functioning socially," and finally, "sometimes I just cry."

When we take a close look at this "fear of being hurt," on the surface it doesn't seem like there is much of a link to thug love because being hurt by a bad boy is practically a certainty—almost as likely as taking your next breath of air. So the obvious question is why women would fear something in a relationship that they are pretty sure will happen anyway. Once again, it sounds like a case of women not taking the time to carefully and methodically think through what this heavily used phrase really means.

All of this would be considered reasonable analysis and conjecture if this fear is directed at bad boys. But suppose this "fear of being hurt" is not directed at bad boys but rather at the not-so-bad boys—the good guys. You read it correctly! A reasonable person could easily consider this a strange way of thinking, but it turns out that "the fear of being hurt" is just that—more directed toward a conventional-type good guy relationship. So the woman avoids going out with "Mr. Right" because he *may* hurt her and turns around and goes out with the bad boy who *will* hurt her. Before you think I'm making this stuff up, look at what Joanne Truner writes in her Internet article "Why Good Girls Choose Bad Boys":

> The first thing I discovered was that I was afraid. I was terrified of finding Mr. Right and being his Ms. Wrong. This fear was pushing me into shallow relationships with men I knew I would never marry. If I didn't get too attached, I couldn't get too hurt.

These are words from a woman who has actually experienced thug love. After reading this, I thought, *What have I gotten myself into?* This is absolutely illogical. I realized that I have two marks against me in trying to understand this one. First, I was a man, and second, I was a psychologist. None of what I just heard registered in my framework of thinking and training. And to make things worse, several women in various discussions regarding this statement actually confirmed that many women really do think like this. I guess this was my "men are from Mars, women are from Venus" moment.

In attempting to decipher what appeared to be some serious contradictory and abnormal thinking, something kind of jumped out at me and said, "Slow down, not so fast." It was like when football referees go to the sidelines and check the videotape of a challenged call and returns to the field and says, "Upon further review," so forth and so on. What came across or appeared to be something utterly irrational from my male point of reference, upon further review, may very well be reasonable thinking from a woman's perspective. In fact, it actually turned out this way.

Male readers may have to do a double take on what you are about to read regarding a woman's fear of being hurt, but this is how it works. Research uncovered that the "fear of being hurt" is one of the most consuming thoughts on a woman's mind. There is little doubt about this. This fear is so prevalent that women engage with bad boys because they know deep down inside that they will never get close enough to them to really get hurt by them. Remember what Joanne Truner said: "If I didn't get too attached, I couldn't get too hurt." A relationship with "Mr. Right" is almost always more than just an emotional one. In fact, it is the multifaceted connection that makes him "Mr. Right." And this is the type of relationship that if it doesn't work out will hurt and hurt deeply if you listen carefully to what women say on this subject. Even with this, getting involved with bad boys to avoid the possibility of being hurt by good guys seems to run so contrary to what women say they want the most in a relationship—a connection, security, and stability.

Fear is one of those emotions that can come from any direction. Fear can come from experience, it can be handed down, and it can even be the result of misinformation. In all of these cases, one thing for sure is that fear is learned behavior. This makes it so difficult to investigate thoroughly because it is the source of the fear that must be identified before help can be on the way. Fear from past experiences is the easiest to deal with because there is something concrete to work with. For example, a lot of women fear mice or spiders. A mouse is something physical, something that is concrete; you can see it and touch it—well, maybe not touch it. Nonetheless it is this type of concrete experience that can be used as an image in fighting the fear. Fear that is handed down is a little more difficult to discern because it usually is based on someone else's experience. This is especially true with women because they tend to bond with each other on an intimate and emotional level which far exceeds anything men would do. Most of us have seen this frequently play out with the female gender. A group of girls get together and more often than not they share their relationship experiences. Men are almost always the number one topic of discussion among women. In these settings, it is inevitable that one or more of the discussions will involve some heartbreaking stories. You know how it ends—"Girl, don't ever let your man do this, or say that, etc." As this occurs, we now have fear that has been handed down. And it should be mentioned that because of the highly sensitive nature of women's friendship, they take each other's advice very seriously. Just try telling most women not to pay attention to her girlfriends and see the look you get. The problem with handed-down fear is that there is no mouse here, nothing tangible or concrete with which to target in developing strategies to remove the fear. Finally, the most complex fear to deal with is the one where the experience that caused the fear is misinterpreted. It is most difficult to help a person navigate through this type of learned behavior because it is based on false premises and invalid assumptions. A good illustration is the challenge attraction, where many women believe that good guys are not exciting. As a result, they turn to bad boys based on invalid assumptions and end up living in abusive and demeaning relationships. The resolution to this problem is to always assess and evaluate experiences based on facts and nothing more.

Fear paralyzes. It keeps you from moving forward or in any direction for that matter. But of course, moving forward is our only goal. So how does the "fear of being hurt" relate to the three reasons that women are attracted to bad boys? Exactly how does the fear factor keep women from moving forward and conquering thug love?

In the protection attraction, the fear factor keeps the woman from moving forward because she is locked in a world where her movements are largely under the bad boy's control. She is paralyzed. And remember that she got under his protection and control because she feared Mr. Right's protection more. In the "a challenge" attraction, the fear factor keeps the woman from moving forward because her appetite for danger and excitement in her relationships has confined her to a world of sex, drugs, and abuse. Here, the woman decides to put up with such horrific personal violations with the bad boy because she fears that the good guy will treat her well and she really doesn't deserve it. And in the "I can fix him" attraction, the fear factor keeps the woman from moving forward because her view of who really needs to be fixed is distorted. The fear of failure almost certainly contributes to the women's distorted view in that if she can't fix him, then she fails, which is seen as not fixing herself. The fear of failure then becomes the fear of being hurt and is strongly related to not being good enough.

So what does all this mean? Well, once again and unfortunately, the fear factor is a feather in the bad boy's cap because they know exactly how to use this fear to prey on women. And we must not forget—it is not the fear of the bad boy.

CHAPTER 13

The Seed Factor

Sex to women is personal while sex to men is physical. While this is not an absolute, it was hard to find women who didn't agree with this premise on some level, and not just women in thug love. Straight talk says that intimacy is so powerful that it ultimately becomes another form of control that bad boys in particular use over their women. From the psychological perspective, many women process intimacy in such a manner that it produces a mindset, and subsequently behavior, that results in an uncontrollable sense of attachment. This intense state of attachment often overlooks cheating, abuse, and other violations in the relationship—largely to avoid what basically comes down to losing or not having a man at all. What else could reasonably explain why so many women in thug love stay in these self-worth–robbing arrangements?

Late in the research, I was discussing my theory of how intimacy affects women to a small group of women. When I described it as an "uncontrollable attachment," Sandra, an African American woman in her late twenties, said, "Oh, you mean d——notized." This is noticeably a play on the word *hypnotized*, which obviously is being used by Sandra to describe some women as being in a trance-like state as it relates to the effects of intimacy. The women in the group all nodded in agreement. It was clear that this was womanspeak and that they were familiar with this term because there wasn't the customary smiles and laughs that usually follow such novel-type statements. I don't recall hearing such a creative expression before, at least from the lips of a woman so openly and candidly. Nevertheless, this surely verified that my theory was on point. How powerful is intimacy, you ask? How well entrenched is sex into the psyche of most of today's women? Well, in all three of the reasons women are attracted to bad boys, intimacy is at the center of the relationship.

In the protection attraction case studies, the term *swag* is used in describing a primary attractive characteristic of the bad boy. At the end of the day, this is a reference to him being sexy. Take off the *y* and what do you have? In the first encounters of the challenge attraction, you may recall I asked in a group discussion if excitement could mean going to an amusement park or something of that nature, and a frustrated young lady said, "Excitement is having wild sex, and I don't know why everybody is trying to put on a front." And in the "I can fix him" case studies, Kelli acknowledges that "the sex was very good" while for Christie, "All we did was have sex every day, sometimes several times a day." Kelli would later say, "Screw it! I'm a woman, and I have needs, and I know where to get it, and it's good, and if I can just, like, turn the volume down on the emotional side of this, I'll be alright." First, it seems clear that she is struggling with this issue. But notice that "turn the volume down on the emotional side" is an attempt to avoid dealing with many of the psychological issues that having sex brings with some women. These are usually recurring thoughts that are very difficult to remove, such as *Is he being faithful? Does he really love me? Is he texting other women? What if I get pregnant?* and so on. Turning down the volume also means escaping the uncontrollable sense of attachment that frequently comes with intimacy. And the attachment is so dominant that it renders many women unable to make rational judgments as it relates to their interpersonal conduct. The power of intimacy in shaping behavior seems to have no equal, especially in thug love. Once intimacy begins, realistic and judicious thinking ends. Therefore, in the classical sense, the theory is that intimacy in bad boy relationships leads to irrational thinking and behavior. Thus, we have "the seed factor." A few case summaries illustrate exactly how powerful a role intimacy plays in real time.

First, Katherine, a young African American lady in her midtwenties, who happened to be married, shared the fact that her bad boy husband left her for another woman and relocated to a different state. About a year or so later, he returned with the idea of trying to make the marriage work. There was one little problem, however: he had the name of the woman he left his wife for tattooed on his arm, and to make matters worse, he was still communicating with her off and on.

Second, Deitra, an African American woman in her early forties, was at home taking a shower getting ready for a romantic evening while her male friend, who had just returned from a long trip, was sitting on the couch supposedly waiting for her. Apparently, he didn't notice that she had completed her shower and turned off the water because when she did, she heard him talking on the phone making rendezvous plans later on that evening with another woman.

Third, and finally, a group of young ladies were discussing going out for dinner after class. One of the women, Judith, a black woman close to thirty years old, said that she didn't think her boyfriend would let her go. It was the "let her go" that grabbed my attention to that conversation. She revealed to her classmates that he drives her to school and picks her up after every class. Nonetheless, she said she was going to try. She went to the car to let him know what she wanted to do and he went ballistic, publicly ballistic. It was very embarrassing. He got out of the automobile and literally escorted her into the car. There is no way I could make this stuff up.

While each of these cases is different in nature, they all had one thing in common: sex was at the top of their list with respect to importance in their relationship. And it was the effects of intimacy, that uncontrollable sense of attachment that was behind all three of these women staying with these guys, in spite of such appalling relationship violations. In fact, the young lady whose husband tattooed the other woman's name on his arm called and asked if I would be disappointed in her if she went back to him. I explained to her it's not my call to make. It is my practice to avoid giving such specific and direct advice, especially in interpersonal relationships. But what I try to do is get the person to critically appraise and think through their situation. To this end, I simply asked her, "Do you think you could live with a man who has another woman's name tattooed to his arm while he was in a relationship with you?" The short story is that they ended up getting a divorce.

After hearing such heart-wrenching stories, and many more for that matter, I couldn't help but think what could possibly be the driving force behind such obvious naiveté. Why can't women in thug love see that this is such a dangerous and totally unrewarding lifestyle? If this is mainly intimacy driven, what are the geneses of this behavior? What do these guys have to make a women behave in such a manner? The short answer, especially to this last question, is that what these guys have is the "seed."

Here is how the seed factor works. In the actual act of intercourse, the man leaves a part of him—his seed—in the woman. To be clear, in many women's mindset, this means that a part of her man is in her body. Conversely, the woman does not leave anything inside the man as a result of intercourse. This is where it gets real personal for the woman and only physical for the man. For the woman, the seed is something tangible, something concrete, and something which marks the event. One the other hand, the man doesn't have any such tangible sign of the act and therefore is less likely to feel a personal connection, especially on the level that the woman feels. Notice that intimacy from the women's perspective is referred to as an event, and from the male perspective, it's an act. By the way, if the man does not leave a physical seed behind because he or the woman uses one of the various methods of protection available these days, he surely leaves a psychological seed. And make no mistake about it: sometimes this can be just as bad for the woman.

A considerable amount of dialogue on this topic was quite revealing as it provided a well-defined picture of how this plays out in real-life action. On average, after a meaningful intimate encounter, the typical woman wants to savor the moment, cherish the event. This may mean cuddling, prolonged embracing, or just plain enjoying quiet time together. Some women have voiced it as "I just want him to be with me." This is the personal! In contrast, from the very lips of many women, far too many guys after an intimate encounter often seem distant relative to the woman. Some immediate after-intercourse personal experiences of women included their guys playing their Xbox's, watching a football game or other sporting event, getting on the computer, or going out and playing a game of pickup basketball with their male friends. This is the physical! A quick related note here is that in the group discussion mentioned earlier, Sandra made it known that when her bad boy went to play the Xbox after their intimacy, she said, "And it was *my* Xbox." In her *Psychology Today* Internet article "Why Do Women Fall for Bad Boys," Vinita Mehta's research seems to confirm what many women in thug love said on this matter: "It is believed that narcissism may advance short-term mating in men, as it involves 'a willingness and ability to compete with one's own sex, and to repel mates shortly after intercourse."

Because of the power of the seed factor, the connection women feel with males they have been intimate with is extremely difficult to break. The psychology alone of such powerfully perceived events ensures that the woman will not forget the event or the connection. It leaves the woman with a tangled web of emotions that is most difficult to sort out and even more difficult to remove. Just try removing all the parts of a plant from the soil where deep roots have developed and you will realize just how difficult this can be. In large part, this accounts for why woman allow men, especially the bad boys, to get away with violating and misusing them because removing them is just like removing that plant—it is a tedious task, but more importantly, it is a psychological task.

When putting the seed factor to the test, nearly seven out of every ten women agreed with the theory. This was especially true with the distinction made between the genders regarding the personal and the physical viewpoint of intimacy. Some women said they liked the fact that I presented this issue as the seed factor because it made them realize that sex can affect so many aspects of a relationship. Also, through exploring the seed factor, it became clear just how far apart a lot of men are from women when it comes to intimacy and having a connected and meaningful relationship.

Finally, if it's personal, then it most likely has been personalized. At the very least, intimacy represents a special bonding, a special link, a special union, and a very exceptional connection to the woman. Breaking this bond is nearly impossible. Most men don't have a clue as to the seriousness of this unique connection which rests in the psyche of the woman. This is evident when quite a few men refer to women's emotions relative to bonding and connection as bizarre or "all that's not necessary." Some women have reported that men have actually gone so far as to say that "they [the women] have lost their minds."

The events of intimacy in the above stories have become a part of these women's psyche, their consciousness, and, more importantly, their unconsciousness. And it's the special nature of these types of events in particular that tend to make women territorial, sometimes to the point of obsession. Here they feel a sense of entitlement in which their attitude is that since they gave themselves, their mind, and particularly their bodies, their bad boys belong to them. Of course, we know this is far from the way it usually turns out. In fact, just think about all that we have learned regarding these volatile relationships, and then consider a bad boy belonging to a woman. Not happening! Not even close to happening! Nonetheless, this territorial mindset is steadfast and drives the irresponsible behavior that often plays out in the relationship. Let me put it like this: once a woman becomes intimate with a man, and especially if the intimacy is satisfying, the odds of her voluntarily leaving him are slim to none! Actually, the odds of her involuntarily leaving him are not much better. Thus, in many cases, women in thug love, and sometimes women in non–thug love relationships, will not leave their man in the face of being controlled, being cheated on, being manipulated and exploited, and even being abused. And a major contributor to this irresponsible and irrational behavior is likely to be the seed factor.

CHAPTER 14

The Chooser/Choosee Factor

It's positional! Whatever stage or position we are in at any given time in life impacts how we think, respond, and ultimately behave. A person in a position of power generally gets more respect than those in positions with little or no power. Additionally, the person who is more highly respected is more likely to feel better about him- or herself as opposed to the person who receives little or no respect. And those in positions of power often have the authority to choose, making many of the major decisions that shape how our society functions. On the interpersonal relationship scene, the man is in the position of power because he gets to choose the woman. This is simply how it is in our culture, and it plays out every day in conventional and nonconventional relationships alike. In thug love, this is the perfect arrangement from which bad boys get to feel good about themselves. This same perfect arrangement, however, is not as kind to women. The woman is left to deal with the social norm of having to be chosen, which in effect stacks the deck against her having a healthy sense of self-worth, especially when dealing with people of questionable intent. What appears to be a perfect arrangement for the bad boy is more of a perfect storm for the woman.

Having to be chosen is like being on a waiting list. In today's society of instant gratification, waiting to be chosen for almost anything can be a mentally challenging and draining experience. Intrinsically, nothing can be as stressful and demeaning as having to wait for someone to select you in order to be engaged in an interpersonal relationship—something that most people take for granted and nearly everyone desires. The positional status of the choosee is not only aggravating but can also have serious psychological consequences— the choosee being left on the waiting list for long periods of time or not being chosen at all comes to mind for starters. Nevertheless, the probable psychological scenario resulting from the women being in the choosee position starts with anxiety, which leads to self-doubt, which leads to problematic behavior. In the land of thug love, this cultural and social dynamic is often followed by acts of desperation. This almost certainly leads to the woman's willingness to accept nearly any type of guy or any type of treatment to get off the waiting list and become one of the chosen. Bad boys have just enough savvy to spot these symptoms and begin to prey on women who they sense are dealing with these low self-worth issues. And in the process, these guys use their positional status to control and manipulate the relationship. With this in mind, Cassandra Mack, in her Internet article entitled "Strategies for Empowered Living," writes:

> If you are in a relationship with a guy who lies, cheats, talks down to you or mistreats you in any way then regardless of what you may want others to believe you do not feel good about yourself.

The chooser/choosee factor plays a prominent role in advancing the thug love attraction. And since it is largely based on positional and situational dynamics, there is little chance the impact of this factor can be avoided. But this doesn't mean that some women wouldn't try to rationalize or outright deny that men had positional power over them. In quite a few conversations along the way, this is exactly what happened. Women would inevitably point out that they also have a position of power within this theory because they can reject the chooser. More often than not, this opinion was argued in a defensive manner; nonetheless, each time it was mentioned I agreed with the women's assessment on this point. Be that as it may, I would always quickly remind them that there would be no rejection without the chooser first exercising his positional status to make the initial selection of the choosee.

Another interesting dynamic within this theory is that a woman who doesn't have problems being chosen often believes that it's less likely she will be disrespected by her bad boy because she was chosen by him. Not so! In fact, her plight could easily be less rewarding or satisfying than the woman who either didn't get chosen or was on the waiting list for a longer period of time because the evidence plainly shows that thug love is almost always a temporary arrangement. Consequently, after the start of a bad boy relationship, it usually won't be long before the chosen becomes the unchosen. The emotional investment is more substantial and therefore will most likely have a much worse psychological affect than not being chosen at all, or being on the waiting list for long periods of time. Going from the top to the bottom, from high to low, from first to last, and from chosen to unchosen can be tantamount to a traumatic experience, especially when in the process the person is being disrespected, cheated on, or abused.

The magnitude of the impact of the chooser/choosee factor is startling if we just remember that anywhere from 70 to 80 percent of women—all women—have reported that they either had a bad boy experience at some point in their lives or were presently in such a relationship. This means that nearly every woman reading this book knows from firsthand experience exactly how it feels to have their self-image demeaned and played with as though they were toys, and the relationship was a game. They understand the emotions associated with being the choosee, and some even understand the psychology of these experiences. But in order to use these incidents to remove the

Help Wanted signs, as always, a deeper understanding of the origins of this behavior must be explored. This left me with several essential questions. How and where does negative self-worth begin within the context of the chooser/choosee factor? What are some of the initial causes of the mindset that allows a woman to accept mistreatment, and worse yet feel that she doesn't deserve better? Somewhere along the way, a door was opened where doubt was allowed to creep in and disarm the rational frame of mind. So when and where did this happen? Under what conditions did the event or events occur in the woman's life that caused such self-destructive conduct?

After considering these questions for a while, I would always remain cognizant of my central beliefs as a researcher that all behavior has a genesis, and I would always look for real-life experiences to sort out questionable behavior. With this, I knew I needed to go to a place where men go to meet women and women go to meet men—a place where I have the best chance to see how the chooser/choosee factor plays out in real time. One of my favorite places to conduct such genuine observational research is the bar scene at mid- to high-end restaurants where some very interesting interpersonal activity usually takes place between men and women. Since I have done this on quite a few occasions, I knew exactly where I would go.

As I entered the restaurant chosen for this observational research, I made sure that I got a seat in a discreet location, but one where I could see the entire bar. After canvassing the scene, one of the first things that I noticed was many of these guys around the bar fit the bad boy profile. But for that matter, some of the ladies could possibly fit a "bad girl" profile as well. I began paying very close attention to see if I could observe any behavior between the sexes that would offer a deeper understanding of how the process of women being chosen by men plays out emotionally and psychologically.

Right about that time three young ladies walked in and sat at the bar. They were pretty attractive women so I decided to focus on them for a while since an attractive group of women tend to grab men's attention rather quickly. They appeared to be in their late twenties to early thirties. As women often do, they were having a lively discussion among themselves, but you could tell they were very cognizant of what was going on around them—that is with respect to men. I'd say about ten minutes had passed and this rather handsome young man, who appeared to be in his mid- to late thirties, took a seat at the bar adjacent to the three ladies. After about ten minutes, he approached the ladies, introduced himself, and began talking to all of them at first. After a little while, say fifteen to twenty minutes, he began to focus in on the one that he apparently wanted to talk to the most. He was able to get her to go to another area of the bar to have a private conversation. My attention was not on the young lady and the guy but rather the reaction of the two ladies who were left behind, or, I should say, not chosen. It was very obvious from their facial expressions and other body language cues that the two remaining women, at the very least, were wondering why their girlfriend was chosen and they were not. I said to myself, "There it is." While this was not the first time I observed this type of social interaction, it would not be my last. In fact, I must have observed this positional scenario play out dozens of times since focusing in on this with respect to the chooser/choosee theory. As always, I had to put this to the test, and in every group discussion, the majority of women consistently confirmed that my facial expression and body language reads were right on the money. Most of them said there was very little doubt that this was what the women were thinking while others were open and candid enough to indicate that they would have surely wondered *Why her and not me?* themselves. I said to one group, "How do you balance this emotionally considering it is one of your girlfriends?" One young lady said, "Do you realize how competitive women are?" I figured I'd better leave that one alone.

The significance in observing how the chooser/choosee factor plays out in real time is that we can see exactly how the door of uncertainty is opened. And once that door is opened, a chain reaction of emotions is triggered. Based on group discussions with women, the women in the observational research who did not get chosen will most likely check and recheck their outfit, their makeup, their hairdo, and so on. When the doubt creeps in, all types of introspection questions will be asked: *Was I too fat/too skinny/too tall/too short?* are just a few of the questions that women are likely to ask themselves when the door of doubt is opened at the hands of the chooser/choosee factor.

CHAPTER 15

Conquering The Fear Factor

The fear is real, but the reality is not. This is not a play on words but a remarkable truth uncovered about the link between fear and thug love. From what we have learned from our investigation, the reality is that while fear has definitely been associated with bad boy relationships, the evidence suggests that this fear is not directed at the bad boy but rather at the good guy. This is why the fear is real, but the reality is not—what sometimes seems real on the surface does not always manifest itself in life's experiences. The first step in conquering this phobia is to understand and fully comprehend that the fear factor is not experienced within thug love but right outside of it. Actually, within this trend, most women run to the bad boy in an effort to evade the good guy. This is a good time to refresh our memory on Joanne Truner's reflection when she said, "The first thing I discovered was I was afraid. I was terrified of finding Mr. Right and being his Miss Wrong."

What do good guys have, and what can they do to cause such emotional stress and instability in women? Well first, it seems they are called good guys because they apparently have done some good and positive things in life—a good education, a good job, and oftentimes a good, stable, and respectful state of mind towards women. We also know that they are usually in a position to provide those things that women really want or, better still, need. Such things include real protection such as a roof over their heads, a sensible and nonabusive approach to adventure and excitement in the relationship, a stable and levelheaded lifestyle that doesn't need fixing—you get the picture. The problem is that these things can be taken away. They are tangible and concrete. They represent stability and security. And in the woman's mindset, having these things taken away is much more painful than anything a bad boy can do. Remember, there is little or nothing tangible and concrete that is offered or invested in bad boy relationships. As Joanne Truner put it, "if I didn't get too attached, I couldn't get too hurt."

One of the major problems with being afraid of being hurt by the good guy is *How does a woman know which good guy, if any, is going to her hurt?* What is the basis of this belief? Nobody really seems to know. Even in the face of repeated inquiries, nothing definitive has surfaced. Nevertheless, the obvious answer is she can't know for certain, which suggests that the woman is willing to believe that most good guys are going to hurt them. But if this belief is based on anything other than facts, such as a personal experience, it is questionable at best. And even if the fear is based on personal experience, you feed the fear when you allow a personal experience to put you in harm's way as dealing with bad boys will do. Imagine how many good and wholesome relationships women have missed out on as a result of the fear factor. It comes down to this: would you rather have a nearly certain hurt with the bad boy or only the possibility of a hurt with a good guy? Unfortunately, far too many women select the bad boy. This is unacceptable thinking if we are going to remove the risky behavior of thug love and replace it with responsible behavior. So here is how we are going to change this irrational thinking. We confront the "fear of being hurt." While you can't be certain which good guy will hurt you, you can surely come close by being armed with the right tools to prevent this from happening as best as possible.

Three things you can do to conquer the fear factor. The first thing you must learn to do is *read before reacting.*

The selection and acceptance process is most critical in minimizing your chances of falling into the grasp of the fear factor. Even though in most cases the woman is chosen, she does in fact have to accept the man who chooses her. Who you select to be your man says a lot about you, how you think, and, moreover, how you respond to your thinking. In the first class of each semester, I have my students engage in a psychological profile activity. Around midsemester, I conduct a second profile activity which will help them gauge their progress in this very important psychological exercise. The purpose of this activity is twofold: First, it shows you can tell a lot about a person by what they say or do through the power of higher-level thinking. In essence, it lets you know what kind of person you are dealing with. Secondly, the level of character and personality insight these exercises provide can be used to make smart choices about dealing with people. Oftentimes we miss very important clues, verbal and nonverbal, about the character of a person because we just don't want to take the time to think on an analytical and critical thinking level. Some think it's a waste of time while others feel it's too complicated. But by not doing so, we are almost certainly inviting relationship grief by making bad choices as a result of not paying close enough attention to the details; in this case, the details of a person's words and deeds. A lot of perceived fears about people can be squashed by getting a good read on a person. Even the police perform psychological profiles on people to get a reasonable picture of what type of criminal they may be dealing with.

In each profile activity, various comments or sayings are used which are very suitable for this type of learning experience. In the initial class, one of the comments I use quite frequently is "I came here with nothing and I still have a little left." After presenting this statement, I then ask, "Using one-word descriptions only, what type of person would make such a statement? What can we tell about this person from his or her words?" In every case, the viewpoints and responses are all over the place. But that's to be expected without any prior training or insight into the principles of psychological profiling. One of the main reasons for the conversation being all over the place is that students begin to restate what has been said so that it fits into their own perspective. Of course, it is pointed out to them that this is not allowed because changing what the person said means we now have a different comment. When students try to do this, I call it "comfort zone processing." To do an adequate assessment, you can only profile what is before you. As we move forward, the most frequent responses usually say that this person is "positive," "truthful," "a believer," "sad," "angry," "a dreamer," and so on. I then have them break the statement down into two parts. I ask them what the main subject of the first part of the statement is. What is the person talking about? The obvious answer is "nothing." I then ask, "What is the subject of the second part of the statement?" And here is where I get all kinds of comfort zone responses, mostly way off base. Nearly 99 percent of the time, I have to provide the answer which is once again "nothing." In the second part of the sentence, the person is referring back to the first part, which is "nothing." The look on the students' faces tells it all, when most of their expressions are saying, "How did I miss that?" I then proceed with my analysis which is simply that two nothings generally equal a double negative, which could easily be argued that at the least, in this statement, the person was projecting a negative attitude. He or she will most likely see many things in life from a negative perspective—probably a person who views life as the glass being half full. So what does this exercise have to do with bad boys? Well, if this same process of analytical thinking in profiling is used by women in accepting the chooser's offer to engage in a relationship with them, then they could cut their chances of making a bad decision tremendously—leaving them with a much better chance of picking a low-risk, high-potential man. I guess I should add a "good guy" man.

Secondly, you must learn to *participate, not anticipate*. If you put your focus on making the relationship a positive and fruitful experience, there will be no time to anticipate something going wrong. That's the response that fear provokes and the response we don't want. It puts the woman in a mode of anticipating the worse. Since fear paralyzes, nothing can be achieved, and you can't move forward. A good dose of involving yourself in the relationship can put fear on the run—so far in the background that it becomes a nonfactor. Instead of waiting or even expecting something negative to happen, play a more active role and help plan an exciting weekend, for example—go to the movies or an amusement park or a dinner at a nice restaurant. Instead of wondering if he is going to call you, be proactive sometimes and call him. And if you are one of those people who feel that being a little proactive will make you look pressed, then you are in the wrong business. And if your guy, or girl for that matter, views your being proactive as being pressed and not trying to advance the relationship, then he or she is the wrong person. Participating means just that—you must be actively engaged in every aspect of the relationship. As long as you are participating on a regular basis, you minimize, and for that matter could outright negate, the chances of your relationship going downhill as a result of fear.

The final nail in the coffin of fear is you must learn to *"ebb and flow."* There is no relationship that will not have problems—disagreements, misunderstandings, and even arguments. This is a natural process in interpersonal interactions. You have gained the insight to be able to read before reacting, and therefore, you are confident that you have selected a man of good character and personality—exactly the kind you are looking for. You are committed to participating and not anticipating, therefore, "ebbing and flowing" is not only a piece of cake, but it can be fun, and, even more significantly, it can be rewarding on many levels.

"Ebb and flow" is basically an attitude of give and take. Both partners learn a lot about their significant other as well as themselves when they share this mindset—and the relationship grows and becomes stronger in the process. And by the way, the fear factor becomes even more of a remote concept when "ebb and flow" is set in motion. An open conversation between you and your man about what constitutes "ebb and flow" would be very beneficial at or near the start of a relationship. When the first major problem arises, both parties will participate in working through the solution. However, no one party will get their way exclusively. For example, the woman wants to go to the movies while the man wants to watch the football game. When your relationship is in full "ebb and flow" mode, the woman agrees to watch the football game first because movie show times are a little more flexible. This will require communication and probably a lot of it. By having this "ebb and flow" mindset, your communication skills increase as well. Another example is that you have a heated argument with your partner. As a result, you guys are not speaking for the moment. This is the type of situation where the "fear of being hurt" can easily reoccur because fear is always lurking around relationships and tends to turn itself up a notch during idle times. However, you now have the tools to defeat this enemy because you have the attitude and mindset of "ebb and flow." And with this mindset, it helps you realize that somebody is going to have to be the first to extend the hand to resolve the issue—perhaps both of you extending the hand at the same time is an even better idea. This becomes an easy thing to do because with your new attitude you understand the importance of give and take in a relationship. After all, there has to be an adult in the room at all times. Correction: with "ebb and flow" at full throttle, it should be said that there has to be adults (with an *s*) in the room at all times.

CHAPTER 16

Conquering The Seed Factor

If anything can mess up a relationship, it would be sex—and it usually does. Since this is the case, one would think that conquering the seed factor would not be that difficult because all the woman has to do is to just stop having sex with her bad boy. This will allow the seed factor to become deactivated in her mindset, and that should pretty much solve that problem of getting out of such unrewarding relationships. Sounds great, but this approach would only work temporarily, if at all, and would most likely have no effect on conquering the seed factor. Human nature tells us that the woman has needs also. Actually, some of the women in our case studies have directly said as much. To stop having sex after months, perhaps even years, with someone whom the woman feels connected and bonded would be a radical change—doable, but radical. Impossible, NO! Improbable, YES! The real focus must be on how the attitude, the thinking, and the mindset were shaped and influenced by intimacy with the bad boy. Critical to this process are the circumstances under which she became connected and bonded because this often reveals the psychological depth of the seed factor. Asking questions and introspection—looking deep inside one's self—are the recipe necessary to achieve the goal of conquering the seed factor in thug love. The only way to adequately accomplish this is by "unsowing the seed." Let me put it this way: we have to cut the umbilical cord, but unlike cutting the umbilical cord of a baby, the thug love umbilical cord must not only be completely cut out but must be replaced as well. Women cringe at the thought of having to do this because so much of who they are and how they see themselves is all wrapped up in their emotions—*intimacy, bonding,* and *connected* are all words that apply here. Nevertheless, if responsible behavior is the goal, you must do this. So let's get on with it!

First, you must unsow the seed of protection, of being dominated, and replant it as the seed of being "direction determined." The absence of a well-planned and directed life often contributes to wanting to be dominated. The bad boy realizes this weakness and tries to create a sense of protection, but in reality, it is a false sense of protection. Of course, we know now it takes a lot more than brute strength to provide you with the real, long-term protection you need—the "roof over your head" type of protection. If truth be told, a woman who is independent and self-reliant can put her own roof over her head. This puts her in a position where she not only doesn't have to rely on a man for protection, she can lower her stress levels as well because she no longer has to worry about losing her security. Conquering the seed factor requires that you to take charge of your life—set goals, put together a strategy, and always function with a purpose. After all, in the end, your "direction determined" attitude and mindset will be your most reliable protection.

Since protection and swagger seem to go together, conquering the seed factor should also include unsowing the seed of being swagger driven and replanting it as the seed of being "substance driven." Swagger is not necessarily a bad thing. A little confidence can be healthy at times. In thug love, however, swagger is considered the premium quality and is often the only quality in the man that matters to a lot of women. Being victorious over the seed factor requires that you look at the inner man rather than the outer man—it's the substance that really matters. A man with financial means and stability, which usually translates to a job and education, can protect you a lot better than a man with macho. Perhaps it should have been said: a man with *legal* financial means, given the nature of this research. Also, a man who is considerate and sharing can make your life a lot more comfortable than a man who is just cool—"cool" serves the bad boy, not the woman. A "substance driven" attitude and mindset will protect you from making bad choices about being protected.

Unsow the seed of seeking "a challenge" and replant it as the seed of seeking "a commitment." We have learned through our study that the excitement and adventure which women gravitate to and use to describe what they mean by "a challenge" is almost always temporary. For the woman who is trying to avoid or change this risky behavior, the quick fix of "a challenge" is unacceptable. Conquering the seed factor requires that you accept nothing less than a tangible, substantive, and devoted relationship. It's all about a firm commitment. There is no greater excitement than knowing you have a man who is committed to you and you alone. There is no greater thrill you can have than sharing quality time with a man who is connected and bonded with you. With an attitude and a mindset where your relationship is all about "a commitment," your replanted seed will produce only the best fruit. Give him the commitment test. What is the commitment test, you ask? Here it is in a nutshell, and this goes for all types of relationships: The best barometer of whether your relationship has a good chance of lasting, whether your relationship is honest and truthful, is for both you and your man to keep your cell phones unlocked and available to your partner at all times. I have shared this relationship measuring method with all types of relationships—heterosexual, bisexual, and homosexual—and less than 2 percent were willing to even consider such an arrangement with their significant other. But the one that takes the cake are married couples where an almost unanimous, sometimes verbal and sometimes nonverbal response was "you have got to be kidding." If you want to know if you are in a committed relationship with your partner, and they won't try the "unlock your cell phone" arrangement, then it would seem reasonable that you have your answer.

Finally, unsow the seed of "I can fix him" and replant it as the seed of "I can fix me!" Control and superwoman issues almost certainly point to insecurity issues. Thus, the fix is on the woman more so than the man. It's not that the bad boy doesn't need fixing, but if you are trying to conquer the seed factor, fixing yourself is much more important. So instead of him being the project, make yourself *the* project. As I mentioned in tip no. 7, taking care of yourself has therapeutic value. This is most effective when you invest in quiet time with yourself. Making and taking the time to be truthful with yourself, gaining ways to get control over and redirect your behavior, and taking the necessary steps to make needed corrections are all ways to help fix yourself and in the process step away from thug love. Unsowing the seed of "I can fix him" will also help you put your real needs in perspective, and once you have been able to make substantial progress in fixing some of your issues, then and only then will you be able to help him deal with his personal issues.

CHAPTER 17

Conquering The Chooser/ Choosee Factor

Okay you didn't get chosen first or second, or worse yet, you didn't get chosen at all. Naturally your feelings are hurt, and you begin to look at yourself and wonder why. Doubt begins to creep in and the next thing you know, your self-esteem and confidence have plummeted to all-time lows. Not feeling good about yourself but looking to fulfill your need to belong has escorted you into thug love. And believing that you deserve no better is instrumental in keeping you there. You begin to realize that your bad boy experience continues to cause your low self-worth issues, and the only way to change this is to step away from thug love. If this sounds like your story or even close to your story, the position you are in may not be your own. And if this doesn't sound like your bad boy story, it most likely is very similar. At any rate, the same holds true—the position you are in may not be your own.

Conquering the chooser/choosee factor is particularly difficult because some parts of the process of how you got there were beyond your control. Once again, "it's positional!" The rules of the game in our society dictate that the man typically chooses the woman. This leaves the woman in the position of having to be selected but, even worse, being in the position to be psychologically manipulated—thus the doubt and low self-esteem. As mentioned earlier, it is highly unlikely that the choosee/chooser rules are about to change in our culture. So how can you conquer this phenomenon if the rules are not going to change? Where there is a will there is a way. If the rules of the game are not likely to change, then you must find ways to change the conditions of how the game is played. There are three things you can do to make this happen: increase the quality of the positional experiences, decrease the quantity of the positional experience, and realign your positional persona.

Increasing the quality of your position simply means upgrading the places you go to to meet guys. Sometimes good guys hang out where the bad boys do. This is due in part because many of them have bought into the notion that good guys come in last. Remember the aforementioned impostor scenario. Conversely, however, you won't find many bad boys hanging out at places where a lot of good guys do. These places tend to stress proper dress—no tank tops, baseball caps, etc. And they tend to maintain an atmosphere that is conducive to interaction on a slightly more well-rounded conversational level. This is good for you because you don't want to take a new attitude to the old places you used to hang out. Not only that, you are making a statement with respect to how you see yourself and what you are willing to accept.

In an interview with a young lady in her midtwenties, she was complaining of having a hard time meeting new guys. Asked what type of places she would go to in hopes of meeting new friends, it became clear the list was very shallow. The idea of a change of venue was discussed as something that could be helpful to her cause. At least this could provide more options. This young lady was pursuing her master's degree online. I asked her had she thought about taking classroom courses, making the point that perhaps this is one way to meet new friends. After thinking it over, the young lady did just that and registered for classes at her local university. She later revealed that while in the process of registering, she saw a couple of guys that were "nice" and in her own description "were smiling all over me." She changed the conditions of her position, and doing so clearly set her up to start conquering the chooser/choosee factor. What did she do? She changed her attitude, her mindset, and her thinking. And by the way, what better place to meet guys, and girls for that matter, than at an institution of higher learning?

Decreasing the quantity of your position is basically reducing, limiting, or just plain eliminating the competition. This seems so simple from the male perspective. You increase your chances of being noticed and therefore selected if you stand out. It's difficult to stand out when you hang out in groups. If you are seriously looking for "that man" and your girlfriend or girlfriends are also looking for the same, you have set yourself up for a higher possibility of rejection and all the other psychological issues that comes with this, much of which has been previously discussed. Why put yourself through that? It is no secret that women are very competitive. Cut your losses! Try to do your own thing, and even if you don't walk away with a man you will at least not walk away feeling bad about yourself because someone else or, worse, one of your own friends was chosen over you. I would be remiss if I didn't mention the fact that going out alone could be a safety issue—especially in these crazy times. But this also depends on the quality of the places you go. If safety is a major issue for you, you can and should at least limit your competition to one friend and not a group of friends. On the other hand, there are places that have security guards and emphasize safety. For the woman who wants to cut the competition and do her own thing, be diligent in this regard. A note of caution about going out alone: some men may read the wrong message in this behavior while other men can be intimated by the woman's independence.

Realigning your positional persona involves dressing for success. This is one of those areas where women are very touchy. That's well and good. Just remember that we are on an upgrade mission, not just psychologically and mentally but physically as well. Dressing for success in this context is the same basic concept usually applied to the workplace. In this case, we are talking about the dating scene. What you wear makes a difference to the type of man you attract. Understanding the male psyche here will give you the heads up with respect to your persona. Sometimes less is more and more is less. Let me use cleavage as an example. A lot of men like to look at a woman's breasts and cleavage—oftentimes the more the better. But here's the twist: they don't want other men looking at their woman's cleavage. What does this tell you about men? This is a problem. Let me state it another way: they like looking at it, but chances are they won't take it home to Mom, especially if it's distasteful. Women reading this book know exactly what I mean. Actually, I think it best for me to say that *most* women reading this book know exactly what I mean. If you are going to realign your positional persona, you want your man to have a sense that you are not on display in that manner for everyone else. Remember how time and time again women knock men because they don't want to bond and feel connected? Well, when a man doesn't want his woman to be on cleavage display—and other types of too-much-information display as well, he has just demonstrated the potential, if not the outright, evidence that he is bondable and connectable in a manner that women say they want and need. At any rate, this is real, and women should consider it when developing their positional persona. I used to always wonder why so many women play their full hand up front anyway. They put it all out there, and then there is nothing left to the imagination—and women are always talking about being bored. The mystery is gone. They play their full hand when only showing some of the cards are necessary to win. This is why getting that self-esteem where it is supposed to be is so important. The better you feel about yourself, the more likely that will be reflected in your appearance. Talk about changing one's attitude, mindset, and thinking; your appearance also changes the way the man thinks about you. Want to get away from the bad boy? Just begin dressing for success on the dating scene.

Chapter 18

Conclusion

The road to discovering why women are attracted to bad boys has taken us in a variety of directions. On some of these roads the path has been straightforward while on others there have been winding streets, sudden turns, and even cul-de-sac–style circles. Risky behavior tends to manifest itself in an array of directions because the very nature of this conduct is random, erratic, and impulsive. But regardless of the various routes that the thug love attraction has taken us, they have ultimately led us back to the only attraction that really matters—the attraction within. The message is consistent yet simple; we must love what's on the inside before we can love what's on the outside. Unfortunately, our tour of the thug love landscape has revealed that a healthy sense of self-worth is practically nonexistent in women who harbor bad boys. And because of this, thug love is able to survive. Most tragic of all is that the absence of love for self has allowed these bad guys to rob women of their personal dignity and integrity by way of disrespect, abuse, and even violence.

This enlightening journey has also exposed the fact that thug love will not allow or promote an inner attraction of love because then it will be defeated. Instead, it advances and thrives on women's insecurities, vulnerabilities, and lack of confidence. The response to this has always been awkward, as well as emotionally and psychologically costly. Until now, the women in thug love have sought to find acceptance without accepting themselves. Until now, the women in thug love have tried to attain respect without respecting themselves. And until now, the women in thug love have tried to experience joy without a song. Nothing communicates better with the soul than a good song. And the soul is where the end of thug love begins. The road that leads to acceptance begins in the soul. The road that leads to self-respect begins in the soul. And the road that leads to joy and freedom from thug love begins in the soul. And what better way to reach the soul than with a song?

The Greek philosopher Plato is often credited with saying, "Let me make the songs of a nation and I care not who makes its laws." While there seems to be no clear evidence that these are indeed the words of Plato, one thing that's clear is this phrase in part is a celebration of the power of song and for good reason because songs, especially inspiring and uplifting songs, come from the soul. They take us to the crescendos of the human experience, while at the same time commanding attention to ourselves and our relationships with each other. The self-help strategies and tips within this book will only take root and become reality if it is channeled through the soul. And this can only be successful with a positive and confident view of self. So what is it about a song that can help a woman in thug love? Well for starters, detaching one's self from these adverse relationships is a soul operation, one that requires a scaffold because the enemy of this phenomenon lies deep within. Not only do songs inspire and uplift; they teach as well. We need to look no further than the three main ingredients of a song. These ingredients speak directly to the soul and therefore teach the fundamental characteristics of self, which is necessary to set in motion the interventions that will lead to productive, stable, and lasting relationships—the kind that most women who have experienced thug love covet.

First, to build a positive self and thus move away from these dignity-robbing relationships, a new sense of independence is required. The melody of a song is generally performed as a single entity and is often treated as the foreground. The beauty of the melody is that as the foreground, it can stand alone. In fact, the melody of a song can be played all by itself and still be recognized and effective. As a woman in thug love sings her new song from the soul, she will in essence develop a sense of independence where she too can stand alone without feeling incomplete. Her melody of independence is liberation from the bondage of needing to be needed.

On the friendship train is where Gladys Knight and the Pips sing "harmony is the key." You won't find a good song without harmony. The study of harmony involves chords and their construction and chord progressions and the principles of connection that govern them. Whether it's harmony within the instrument or vocal family, they work together to produce a very pleasing and soothing sound. There is harmony in the soul. Thug love women just have to find it because the harmony in the soul is where the woman begins to construct the various pieces of a positive and sound mindset that ultimately enhances a positive relationship by blending the two parties together on one accord. When constructing harmony correctly, the end result is almost always perfect peace.

Timing is everything. As the rhythm of the song is absorbed in the soul, the movement of the relationship will be fine-tuned and will prosper at an organized and safe pace. When to start or when to stop can be a matter of success or failure. When to speed up or when to slow down can also be a matter of winning or losing. The rhythms of the world are what keeps everything in sync and thus everything moving forward. So it is with a forward-moving, progressive relationship. When the woman walks in rhythm with her independence, she knows that sometimes, to maintain a good relationship, you might have to accelerate, or sometimes decelerate, or even sometimes simply pause and chill out. A good sense of rhythm will maintain the appropriate pace between both parties, which will keep it moving in a direction where the relationship will prosper.

Finally, the lessons learned are precious and priceless. The Help Wanted signs can now be torn down, and a healthy sense of self and love of self can be realized. This journey of bumpy roads, unclear road signs, and unpaved streets have been repaved and now provide a straight and narrow path to a much higher quality of interpersonal relationships. And thanks to this journey, there is a new compass for acceptance, a new road to respect, and a new song that will direct us to the core of the attraction within—the soul. The victory over thug love is not just a matter of how we feel in our hearts, or how we think in our minds, but more importantly, it is a matter of the soul. It is only in the soul where the woman in thug love will be able work out the usual and always present struggles between her mind and her heart—the battle between what she thinks she should do and what she feels she should do. And make no mistake about it: as the soul acts as an arbitrator between the mind and heart, it will prepare the way for success in changing the risky behavior in thug love to more responsible behavior.

References

Baron, R. & Byrne, D. (2004). *Social Psychology (10 Ed.)* Upper-Saddle River, New Jersey, Pearson Education, Inc.

Bogaert, A. F., & Fisher, W. A. (1995). Predictors of university men's number of sexual partners. *Journal of Sex Research, 32,* 119–130.

Bensley, D. (1998). *Critical Thinking in Psychology: A Unified Skills Approach.* Pacific Grove, CA. Brooks/Cole Publishing Company.

Ciccarelli, S. & White, J. (2012). *Psychology (3rd Ed.).* Upper Saddle River, New Jersey, Pearson Education, Inc., Prentice Hall.

Creswell, J. (2003). *Research Design: Qualitative, quantitative, and mixed methods approaches (2nd Ed.).* Thousand Oaks, CA. Sage Publication.

Daily, L. "Why Good Girls Love Bad Boys." Romantics Network. *http://www.romantics.net/writer/lisa/badboys.html.*

De Ciantis, L. (2014). Women Love Bad Boys: The Psychology Behind Why Women Go For The Assh*les. *Elite Daily.* http://elitedaily.com/women/every-girl-secretly-loves-tucker-max/

Desrochers, S. (1995). What types of men are most attractive and most repulsive to women? *Sex Roles, 32,* 375–391.

Dowd, M. Their Dangerous Swagger, New York Times. Op. Ed., June 8, 2010

Eager, R. (2000). "Why Do Good Girls Date Bad Boys? *http://powertochange.com/experience/sex-love/datingbadboys/*

EHarmony Staff. 4 Reasons women are attracted to Bad Boys. *http://www.eharmony.com/dating-advice/dating/4-reasons-women-are-attracted-to-bad-boys/#.U7_sgbko-M8*

Gay, L. R. & Airasian, P. (2000). *Educational Research: Competencies for Analysis and Application.* Upper Saddles River, New Jersey. Pearson Education, Inc.

Gladding, S. (2013). *Counseling: A comprehensive profession.* (7th Ed.). Upper Saddle River, New Jersey. Pearson Prentice Hall.

Gosselin, D. (2010). *Heavy Hands: An Introduction to the Crimes of Family Violence* (4th Ed.) Upper-Saddle River, New Jersey, Pearson Education, Inc.

Grayson, A. (June 19, 2008) "Why Nice Guys Finish Last." ABC News Medical Unit. http://abcnews.go.com/Health/story?id=5197531

Herold, E. & Milhausen R. 1999. Dating Preference of University Women: An Analysis of the Nice Guy Stereotype. *Journal of Sex & Marital Therapy,* 25; 333.

Hughes, Zondra. (April, 2000). "Why Some Good Girls Prefer Bad Guys." *Ebony Magazine.* Vol. 55 Issue 6, p84. http://connection.ebscohost.com/c/articles/2865107/why-some-good-girls-prefer-bad-guys

Impett, E. A. Peplau, L. A. (2002). Why Some Women Consent to Unwanted Sex with a Dating Partner: Insights from Attachment Theory. *Psychology of Women Quarterly,* 03616843, Vol. 26, Issue 4.

Jensen-Campbell, L. A., Graziano, W. G., & West, S. G. (1995). Dominance, prosocial orientation, and female preferences: Do nice guys really finish last? *Journal of Personality and Social Psychology, 68,* 427–440.

Kinney, J. (2010). *A Handbook of Alcohol Information* (10th Ed.) New York, McGraw-Hill Companies, Inc.

Lesko, W. (2003). *Readings in Social Psychology: General, Classic, and Contemporary Selections* (5th Ed.). Boston MA. Pearson Education, Inc.

Macionis, J. (2012). *Sociology* (14th Ed.). Upper Saddles River, New Jersey: Pearson Education, Inc.

Mack, C. (2000). Strategies for Empowered Living *http://strategiesforempoweredliving.com*

Marano, Hara E. 2005. The Allure of Bad Boys. *Psychology Today*; Jan/ Feb 2005; 38, 1 ProQuest Psychology Journals, pg. 14.

Mehta, V. (2013). Head Games: Why Do Women Fall for Bad Boys? *Psychology Today.* *http://www.psychologytoday.com/blog/ head-games/201310/why-do-women-fall-bad-boys*

Patton, M. (2002). *Qualitative Research & Evaluation Methods (3rd ed.).* Thousand Oaks, CA: Sage Publications, Inc.

Rice, P. & Dolgin K. (2005). *The Adolescent: Development, Relationships, and Culture.* Boston, MA. Pearson Education, Inc.

Sadalla, E. K., Kenrick, D. T., & Venshure, B. (1987). Dominance and heterosexual attraction. *Journal of Personality and Social Psychology, 52,* 730–738.

Shepart, J. & Greene, R. (2003). *Sociology and You.* Columbus, Ohio. Glenco/McGraw-Hill.

Shibley-Hyde, J., & Delamater, J. D. (2000). *Understanding Human Sexuality.* New York: McGraw-Hill.

Sperling, M. & Berman, W. (1994). *Attachment in Adults: Clinical and Developmental Perspectives.* New York, NY. The Guilford Press.

Stack, R. (1995). *The Art of Case Study Research.* Thousand Oaks, CA: Safe Publications, Inc.

Truner, J. (2010). Why Good Girls Chose Bad Boys. Women of Spirit. *http://www.womenofspirit.com/?id=110*

Weiderman, M. W. (1993). Evolved gender differences in mate preferences: Evidence from personal advertisements. *Ethology and Sociobiology, 14,* 331–352.

Zanden, J., Crandell, T., & Crandell, C. (2010). *Human Development* (10th Ed.). New York, NY: McGraw-Hill Companies, Inc.

Weiderman, M. W. (1993). Evolved gender differences in mate preferences: Evidence from personal advertisements. *Ethology and Sociobiology, 14,* 331–352.

Edwards Brothers Malloy
Thorofare, NJ USA
April 17, 2015